BEGINNING STAMP COLLECTING

BEGINNING STAMP COLLECTING
by Bill Olcheski

Henry Z. Walck, Inc., New York

To Rosemary . . .
Patient wife and critic
and the biggest help of all!

Library of Congress Cataloging in Publication Data

Olcheski, Bill.
    Beginning stamp collecting.

    Includes index.
    SUMMARY: An introduction to stamp collecting
with chapters on how to get stamps, picking an album,
first-day covers, and stamp clubs and shows.
    1. Postage-stamps—Collectors and collecting
—Juvenile literature. [1. Postage stamps—
Collectors and collecting] I. Title.
HE6215.047   796'.56'075   74-25978
ISBN Cloth: 0-8098-2429-9

10 9 8 7 6 5 4 3

MANUFACTURED IN THE UNITED STATES OF AMERICA

Designed by Gene Siegel

Acknowledgments

A book seldom is the result of the efforts of only one person. This book is no exception. It is the product of many years of working with people who know and love stamps and with new collectors who want to learn about them.

I am indebted to Herb Harris of the Office of Stamps for the many times he pointed me in the right direction as I sought background information. To Jim Conlon and his staff at the Bureau of Engraving and Printing for careful explanations of complicated processes. To Bill Waugh who started me in stamp collecting and who read over my material with a kind but critical eye. To Nat Grossblat for a review of the chapter on printing and to Franklin R. Bruns, Jr., and Carl Scheele for friendly advice over many years. To Jay Carpenter who has forgotten more about printing than I will ever know.

To my father, who has soaked millions of stamps with me over the years, and to my mother, who put up with the mess in her kitchen. To my mother-in-law, Mary Breslin. To my children, Julie, Bill, Cathy, Sue and Jim, and Jim's buddy Randy Erickson and the many others who looked over bits of the book and gave me their reaction to it. To Victor Werner who prodded me until I finally settled down and wrote the book. To Bernard Haldane who helped convince me I could do it. To all of these and to any others I may have forgotten to mention, my sincere thanks.

Contents

Introduction

You can find a new hobby waiting for you no further away than your mailbox or your nearest post office. It is a hobby you can work at alone or one which you can share with your family and friends. By its fancy name it is known as philately; by its easier name it is called stamp collecting.

It has been the hobby of kings and presidents, of rich and poor. Adults of all ages and millions of children enjoy it.

When you sit down to work on your stamps you will be doing something that other people are doing at the same time at distant places around the globe. Their language may be different from yours, and their albums probably would look strange to you. But they are doing essentially the same thing you are—gathering, sorting, and placing in an album the postal issues of their own and other countries.

Basically, there are three things you need in order to begin a stamp collection. The first is an interest in stamps; the second is some spare time; and the third is a source of stamps. You already have the first or you wouldn't be reading this book. The second is something you can arrange; and the third will be discussed in detail elsewhere in this book.

There are some decisions you will have to make as you embark on your new hobby. These include what you will want to collect and how you will want to go about it. In later chapters we will talk about what to consider in picking an album; the advantages of joining or forming a stamp club; and how stamp dealers can help you get the stamps you want, as well as other things you may want to know.

Stamp collecting probably began in England back around 1840, shortly after the appearance of the first formal stamps. The first United States stamps date back to 1847. No doubt some youngsters began their collections shortly after that time. Think how exciting it would have been to collect during those first years of our postal history. Your collection could have included all of the stamps issued by the United States and you wouldn't need an album with more than two or three pages. To house a collection of all the United States stamps issued since that time would require a massive album with hundreds of pages. The National Stamp Collection, at the Smithsonian Institution in Washington, is mounted under glass in frames and takes up most of the space in a big room. If your travels take you to Washington in future years, be sure to visit the Smithsonian and have a good look at the collection. You'll see stamps there you probably won't ever get a chance to see anywhere else.

While the hobby has been around for a long while, the events featured on United States stamps have kept up with the times. That's why we have stamps today which spotlight the issues which are important in our daily lives. For instance, we have stamps which warn of the dangers of drug abuse, and stamps which encourage us to conserve the wildlife of our country.

Special issues of U.S. stamps show us the flags of our country from the earliest colonial days. Other stamps let us watch the growth of our nation as new states were added to the Union and new stars added to the flag.

Stamps, like those in the Presidential series of 1938, show us the men who have been leaders in our history. Other stamps, like the Famous American Series of 1940, depict men and women who were prominent in fields ranging from education to music, from writing to inventing.

In short, stamps are a kind of mirror which reflects the image of people and events important to us and to our nation.

Popular Subject
The Statue of Liberty appears on a number of United States stamps. This is the eighteen-cent issue of 1973.

There is no need for heavy financial investment as you begin collecting. That's another way of saying you don't have to blow a lot of money on albums and accessories before you can begin to enjoy the fun and excitement of collecting. In fact, it is better to hold down your spending until you have had a chance to decide what and how you want to collect. You then will be able to make wise decisions regarding the kind of albums and other accessories in which you want to invest.

Don't try to move too fast in collecting, although this is a great temptation to the beginner. The first step is to decide that you want to collect. You have taken that step or you wouldn't have read this far. Now, you progress to deciding what you are going to collect—whether you are going to collect United States or foreign; mint or used; old or new; regulars or commemoratives; topicals or other specialties.

You should become aware at this point that stamp collecting has a language all its own, a language in which you are going to have to know at least some of the key words if your collecting is to proceed in a satisfactory fashion. If you are a Scout, look in the handbooks for the stamp collecting merit badge and read its requirements. The handbook gives you some of the terms you need to know. It also sets some standards against which you can measure your progress as a collector.

There actually are dictionaries and other compilations of the words used by stamp collectors. In the early stages of your collecting it is both unnecessary and unwise to burden yourself with all of the technical words. Knowledge and understanding of them will come as you move along in collecting and encounter situations in which you will need to use the different terms.

For now, it is enough to learn just a few of the key words. Since most new collectors begin with the issues of their own countries, let's consider some of the words you will hear in dealing with United States stamps.

Two of the most common terms are "regular" issues and "commemorative" issues. The regular issues, as the name suggests, are stamps which are designed for continued use over a long period of time. They are printed in large numbers and are reprinted whenever the supply runs down. These are the common stamps you see every day. They include the small flag stamps, the Washingtons, Jacksons, and Jeffersons. These stamps generally are smaller in size because they are designed for use by businesses and by people who probably have no interest in stamp collecting.

First Stamp
Benjamin Franklin was featured on the first U.S. postage stamp. It was issued July 1, 1847.

The issues most popular with United States collectors are the ones we call commemoratives. These are the special stamps which mark an anniversary or an event important to the country. These stamps are printed in limited quantities and are not reprinted when the supply runs out. This does not mean that commemoratives will become scarce in a short time. Ours is a big country and uses many stamps each day. When a new commemorative is issued, about 130 million are printed. Of course, not all these stamps end up in the hands of collectors. Most are used up in normal business and personal mail and are thrown away by the recipients.

Thousands of new stamps never carry a letter at all. They are bought from the post office by collectors and placed in an album. Most U.S. stamps continue to be valid for postage indefinitely. Thus you could put an 1893 stamp on your letter today and the letter would be delivered. However, since the value of the stamp would be considerably more to a collector, it is unlikely you would use it for postage.

Stamp dealers gather up hundreds of thousands of used copies of each stamp so they will be able to fill orders from customers when the stamp no longer is in common use. Dealers put so many of the stamps away that most United States stamps are readily available for at least twenty years after they are issued, despite the fact that the U.S. Postal Service reports that there are about 16 million stamp collectors in the United States.

Additional thousands of stamps are used on "first-day covers." We will discuss in detail how to send for them in Chapter Seven, but for now this is what the term means.

When a new United States stamp is released, it comes out in only one city on the day it is issued, generally a city which has some connection with the person or event being commemorated. The next day it becomes available in the more than thirty thousand post offices around the country. Letters carrying the new stamp which are processed in the issue city carry the words "First Day of Issue" in the cancellation lines placed across the face of the stamp.

Envelopes prepared to receive this special cancellation often carry a design related to the event being commemorated. This design appears at the left side of the envelope and is known as a cachet. An envelope with such a design, which has also received a first-day cancellation, is known as a cacheted first-day cover.

It is necessary to request first-day cancellations. The spe-

Regular Issues

The Regular Issue stamps of a country tell us much about the country. These are the first five values in a set of 15 issued in 1967. Regular issues, unlike commemoratives, are designed for use over a long period of time.

cial marking will not be put on ordinary letters mailed during the day in the first-day city, even if they carry one of the new stamps.

In addition to learning the language of stamp collecting, it is important that you become familiar with some of the "tools" used by collectors. One such tool is a set of tongs. Stamp tongs look like the tweezers you see in a manicure set, but there is a big difference. The tweezers often have sharp points. The tongs used by stamp collectors have edges which have been flattened.

Tongs are used to pick up stamps when placing them in an album, moving them from place to place, or when just looking at them. It is not good to touch a stamp, particularly an unused stamp, with your fingers. A bit of dampness on your hand could disturb the adhesive on the back of the stamp and reduce its value to a collector.

Get tongs from a stamp dealer or from a philatelic sales counter. If you get tweezers by mistake, you could end up putting a few holes in the first stamp you pick up.

In the chapters to come we will tell you how to organize your stamp collection and how to use this organization to help you decide the kind of album you will need. You will learn about catalogs and how to use them; about perforation gauges and watermark detectors; about hinges and other methods of attaching your stamps to the album pages.

We will talk about stamp clubs and show you how to get a club started in your school or in your neighborhood. We will tell you how to get new members and how to keep the meetings exciting. We will talk about stamp dealers and the services they offer, and show you what goes into determining the price of a stamp.

You will learn about national groups you can join and about what it is like to attend a stamp show. There will be information about junior stamp clubs and junior stamp shows. There even will be a little history, but not too much, since this is meant to be a "how-to-do-it" book rather than a history book.

In summary, this book will introduce you to the joys and adventures of stamp collecting. It will answer your questions and make it easier for you to explain stamp collecting to adult friends who might be considering taking up the hobby.

While this book is intended primarily for young collectors, you will find adults looking over your shoulder as you get excited about stamp collecting. Later on we will show you how to use that interest to help your own collecting.

The United States Postal Service is more aware of the stamp collector now than at any other time in the history of our country. The Postal Service wants you to be a stamp collector and it will be doing many things to encourage you to start a collection and keep it going. There will be new and colorful stamp issues at regular intervals, some of them in unusual colors, shapes and designs, to attract your attention. You can expect to hear more about first-day covers, stamp posters, and even stamp programs and films in schools.

By beginning now you are getting in on the ground floor of a hobby you can enjoy for the rest of your life. Some special collecting approaches which young hobbyists might want to consider will be discussed in Chapter Six.

Stamp collecting is the hobby of the prince and the pauper; it has something for everyone. Begin today to share in the many rewards it offers for a small investment of your time and money.

Happy collecting!

1
How to Get Stamps

Your sources of stamps to begin your collection depend to some extent on the kind of stamp collecting you want to do. The approach is different, for instance, for getting used stamps than it is for getting unused ones. It is different for getting foreign stamps than it is for stamps of the United States.

Initially, you will probably want to acquire as many stamps as possible, without being too concerned about what type they are or the country from which they come. Later, we will discuss the sorting and separation process which will help you decide what and how you want to collect. For now, let us begin by assuming you are interested in United States stamps which have been postally used—that is, those which have carried a letter. They are the easiest to get and they make a good starting point for collecting.

Begin by making your friends and relatives aware of your interest in stamps. Ask them to save you all of the stamps that come on their mail. Tell them not to worry about duplication.

Have them tear off the corners of the envelopes holding the stamps but warn them not to tear too close to the stamps. Most modern stamps you will encounter have "perforations" around the edges. These are holes which have been put there to make it easier to separate the stamps when you are ready to use them. If the perforations are torn or cut, they destroy any value the stamp may have had for a collector. The same is true if the stamp is "thin." This condition occurs when a person tries to pull a stamp off an envelope and leaves some of the stamp stuck to the paper in the process. The only safe way to remove stamps from an envelope without damaging them is by soaking. This process will be explained in the next chapter.

Check with your parents and grandparents, and ask them if they did any collecting in the past. Somewhere, perhaps in a box in the attic, there could be an old album gathering dust. You just might be able to make this album, or at least some of the stamps in it, the basis for your collection.

Back before the days of television, there were several stamp shows on the radio. One big soap company even put out its own albums for use by listeners to the stamp show.

If you can locate an old album, remove the stamps with care. They may be brittle from being stored many years, or they may be stuck to the pages. Get some advice from an experienced collector before you begin the removal job. Stamps that are stuck require special handling. If nothing else works, the pages can be removed from the album and the stamps soaked off.

Generally, used albums have little or no value. The exception is when the album is very old or unusual. Check with a collector group or stamp dealer before discarding an old album. You might have more of a treasure than you realize.

After you have your friends and relatives saving stamps for you, look around the community and see where else you might find stamp sources. The neighborhood bank, the corner store, city hall, the telephone company—any place which gets quantities of mail is a good place to begin.

You may think every business place has a stamp collector who gathers up all the stamps that come in. This is not usually the case. Many business firms simply throw out their envelopes each day. These discarded stamps could be the start of a good collection for you.

Sometimes you can get business places to save stamps for you by offering them a service in return. Tell a businessman, for instance, that you will be glad to look through his discarded envelopes once a week to be sure that no checks, cash or letters are accidentally thrown out. If you find only one check over a long period of time, you still are saving the merchant trouble and embarrassment and he probably will appreciate your offer and your help.

Don't be concerned if you get a great many stamps of one kind. To reject certain stamps simply because you have many of one variety could be an expensive mistake. For instance, suppose that you are getting the stamps from a bookstore in your area. They may get heavy shipments of books which carry a great deal of postage. Thus you could have an accumulation of five-dollar stamps and might assume they are easy to acquire. In fact, these stamps are very hard for the average collector to get, and they would be valuable regardless of how many you might pile up. Whether you choose to use your duplicates as trading material or decide to sell them to a dealer or another collector, you should be aware of their value.

Up to now we have talked about getting used U.S. stamps without cost to you. Let's look now at the ways in which you can acquire used foreign stamps without putting out any money.

The same suggestions apply that we have outlined for the United States issues. However, the same sources are not as likely to produce foreign stamps so you have to use a bit more ingenuity.

Instead of just checking the local merchants, look in the telephone book and see if there are any consulates, embassies or other foreign government offices in your area. If you are close enough to visit them, do so. They usually keep on hand selections of their stamps which they are happy to give to young collectors. The same is often true of foreign airline offices and travel agencies.

If you can't visit the offices, try calling them. Better still, write a short letter saying you are beginning a stamp collection and would appreciate having a few stamps from their country. You frequently get a bonus in that they will send along some pamphlets or picture post cards from their country. These can help dress up your album when you decide to try some variations later in your collecting.

See if any of your friends have foreign backgrounds or have parents in military or diplomatic service, or have relatives in foreign countries. If so, they may have quantities of foreign stamps they are willing to trade for your U.S. duplicates.

After you have exhausted all of your sources of free

stamps, you must begin to think about buying some for your collection. Don't rush into this step until you have taken all of the other steps outlined here.

The collector who wants unused stamps or used foreign stamps generally has to begin thinking about spending money on them before the collector of used U.S. issues does.

Stamps may be purchased from many places. You can buy them at a post office or from a stamp dealer or another collector. You can buy them in a stamp store or from the stamp department of some of the major department stores. You can visit stamp auctions or bid in mail auctions. You can ship off orders to dealers and postal administrations in distant lands.

Before you do any of these things, think again of the adult friends you have called upon to help you get used stamps. They can be of further help to you in getting unused issues. You probably will have to give them some suggestions on what they can do.

You might want to ask them to be on the lookout for plate blocks for you when they go to the post office. The plate block usually consists of the four corner stamps and the plate number that will be in the margin of each sheet bought from the post office. Be sure to warn them that some of the multicolor stamps have more than one plate number and that it is necessary in such cases to save the entire two end rows of stamps, the row adjacent to the plate numbers and the next one.

In recent years the collecting of "Mr. ZIP" and "Mail Early" blocks has become popular. These blocks generally

Honors from Overseas

Foreign nations often honor American heroes. This stamp from Israel pays tribute to former President Harry S. Truman. A person must be dead before he or she can appear on a U.S. stamp. Living Americans have appeared on stamps of foreign countries.

consist of the four or six stamps nearest the words *Mr. ZIP* or *Mail Early* in the margins of the sheets as they come from the post office.

Smart collectors make regular stops at the post office and get to know one or more of the postal clerks. Ordinarily you have to buy extra stamps to get a plate block. But if you are friendly with the postal clerks, they often will sell you the blocks and then sell the rest of the stamps on the sheet to people who are not collectors and therefore not interested in blocks.

You never will be able to buy U.S. unused stamps any cheaper than you can buy them when they are current at the post office. Therefore it makes sense to get all the new issues as soon as they become available at your local postal station. Not all post offices will stock all issues. If this proves true in your area, you still can order unused stamps at face value for a small service charge from the Philatelic Sales Division of the Postal Service in Washington. The division is located in Postal Service headquarters. It keeps a stock of recent issues—some going back two or more years—for sale to collectors. You can write to the Philatelic Sales Division, whose address is listed on page 130, and request a list of the stamps they currently have available. Enclose a stamped, self-addressed envelope. The list often carries stamps which have not been available in some post offices for several years.

Eventually you will have to turn to the commercial philatelic market as a source for both used and unused stamps. When you do, here are some tips on how to decide where and how to spend your money.

Learn to shop for stamps. Go into several stamp stores and compare their prices for the stamps in which you are interested. Ask them if they have a price list and then take it home and compare it with price lists from other dealers.

One caution at this point: Condition is an important factor in the price of stamps. A stamp which is nicely centered, lightly canceled and without any visible nicks or tears could sell for as much as double the price of a stamp not in such good condition. When dealers and collectors talk about stamps in mint condition, they mean unused stamps with the gum intact as they come from the Postal Service. An unused stamp from which the gum has been washed off is worth considerably less to a collector than one in which the gum is undisturbed. A stamp which has never been hinged usually will sell for more than a stamp which has been attached to an album page. Keep these factors in mind as you compare prices.

A visit to your school or public library will give you an opportunity to look over several stamp publications. If your library does not have philatelic journals, ask them to subscribe to one or more. Also ask them for a list of stamp publications. You can write to the publisher and most will send you a sample copy without charge. You will find the names and addresses of some publications which might interest you on page 130.

When you get the copies, look them over carefully. See what the various advertisers have to offer and see if they meet your specific needs. Compare the offers with prices quoted in other publications for similar material. If you do order by mail, make your first orders small ones. This gives you a chance to get familiar with the dealers' methods, the quality of stamps offered and the pricing system used.

Beware of free offers; they often have a hook attached. An advertisement which offers you a free packet of stamps does so in the hope of getting you to buy stamps from the "approvals" which accompany the free stamps.

Approvals are stamps which are mounted in books with the price under each stamp. You are expected to select the stamps you want and return the others along with payment for the stamps you take. If you write to a company and ask for a selection of approvals, you are obliged to pay for the ones you take and return the others. Failure to do so could involve you—and your parents—in a long exchange of letters and a hassle with postal authorities. It is also dishonest.

Generally, the first approval selection you receive is relatively inexpensive. When you send in your payment, you soon receive a second selection a bit more costly than the first. The lots get progressively more expensive.

Approval buying is just one way of buying stamps. It has the advantage of letting you examine the stamps in your home and make the selections at your own pace. The biggest disadvantage is the cost. The reason for this high cost is explained in the discussion of approvals in Chapter Six.

As your collecting becomes more advanced, you may want to use a system of buying known as a "want list." In the chapter on catalogs (Chapter Five) we will show you how each stamp produced in the world is assigned a number. This number is all you need to identify any stamp you wish to purchase. You send a dealer a list of Scott or Minkus numbers

19th CENTURY COUNTRY STORE-POST OFFICE EXHIBIT
Former post office, Headsville, West Virginia (c.1861-1914)
The National Museum of History and Technolgy, Washington, D.C.

19th CENTURY COUNTRY STORE-POST OFFICE EXHIBIT
Former post office, Headsville, West Virginia (c.1861-1914)
The National Museum of History and Technolgy, Washington, D.C.

A Bit of History

These letters were among the first canceled at the restored post office now located in the Smithsonian Institution in Washington. The post office originally was located at Headsville, West Virginia, and was moved to the Smithsonian. It was rededicated by the postmaster general on September 27, 1971.

and he sends you the stamps you want. The big advantage in this method is that you get only the stamps you want and you don't have to spend time going through approval selections. Once again, the disadvantage is the cost. As we go along in this book, you will learn that the more a stamp dealer has to do for you the more your stamps are going to cost. Want lists rate among the more expensive ways of getting stamps since a dealer may have to hunt through auctions or contact other dealers in order to get the stamps you want.

Many new collectors, particularly those interested in foreign stamps, like to buy stamp packets. If you decide to follow this pattern, always buy the biggest packet you can afford. The temptation is to buy many small packets in the hope of getting a larger variety. The problem here is that the stamps you buy in the smallest packets will turn up again when you buy a larger packet. You are much better off getting a packet of several thousand different stamps than you are if you buy many small packets. Packet buying is really only good for absolute beginners. After that you begin to know the countries and types of stamps in which you are interested and you will want to buy individual stamps and sets.

Foreign stamps of some nations also may be purchased as "kiloware" or "mission mixes." Purchases of this type are explained and discussed in Chapter Eight.

In Chapter Ten we will talk about stamp clubs and the advantages of membership in such a group. An obvious benefit is the opportunity it gives you to meet with other collectors. Collecting with others adds to the fun. It also opens the door to trading your duplicate stamps and swapping information you have gained about how to improve your collection.

For now, concentrate on accumulating all the stamps you can get your hands on. Don't be selective, take everything you can get. The stamps you decide you don't want to keep later on can be used for trading material.

In the next chapter we will show you how to begin to process and organize the stamps you have accumulated.

2
Getting Started

Getting organized is an important part of stamp collecting. It helps you to know what you have and to make wise decisions on how you want to proceed.

Up to this point we have talked only about accumulating stamps and you probably have a pile of them in a cigar or shoe box. You are ready to take the next step before you select an album.

Begin by making a preliminary sorting of the stamps you have. Sorting is fun. It lets you see the stamps you have and you can enjoy looking at them as you go through the separation process. You probably will sort the same stamps over many times during your collecting years.

For this first sorting, put the stamps that are attached to paper in one pile and those that are off paper in another. We will concentrate first on the ones that are on paper.

These stamps will have to be removed from the paper in order to prepare them for mounting in albums. There are a number of ways in which this can be done. The stamps can be steamed off; they can be removed with special kits which introduce limited amounts of moisture and cause the stamps to separate from the paper; or they can be soaked off. Soaking is by far the fastest, least complicated and least expensive of all the methods.

There is one preliminary step before you are ready to begin the soaking process. Go through and remove any stamps which are attached to brightly colored paper. Such paper tends to "run" or release color when it is wet. This could cause a stain which would attach to your other stamps and diminish their value to a collector.

Think small as you approach the soaking process. Get a small pan, a pile of newspapers and a pair of tongs. The only other thing you need is a supply of patience. Moving too fast can create problems.

Put perhaps two dozen stamps in the pan of water. Put them in face down. Use cool or warm water, not hot. Some stamps are printed in soluble inks and hot water could cause them to fade. After a few minutes the stamps will begin to separate from the paper. The stamps will sink to the bottom of the pan, the paper will float. Use the tongs to remove the paper and discard it.

Some stamps will continue to stick to the paper. Move them around in the water and give them more soaking time. Never try to peel a stamp from the paper. This could result in a "thin," as explained in the first chapter. Use the tongs to remove stamps from the water. Give them a little extra rinse to remove any excess gum. This is important because gum left on the backs will cause the stamps to curl when they are drying. Allow the excess water to drain off before you take them out of the pan.

When the stamps are removed from the water, they should be placed face down on a newspaper to dry. Do not use the comic section or any pages which have colored advertisements as the wet stamps could cause the colors to run and stain the stamps. You can avoid this by using paper towels to dry the stamps but this is an extra expense, and unnecessary if you are careful. Stamps which crease or stick to the newspaper in the drying process can be resoaked.

Once a batch has been soaked, repeat the procedure until all of the stamps have been processed. After two or three batches, it is a good idea to change the water as the dissolved gum begins to accumulate. When the water starts to turn yellow it is a sign that it should be changed.

After the stamps have been spread on the newspaper, give

them enough time to dry. Leave them overnight if possible. The dried stamps should be pressed down until they lie flat. An old telephone book works very well for this purpose. Put the stamps between the pages and put a weight on top. In about a day the stamps will be ready for further processing.

The sorting process is a separate venture and it is best approached on a day when there is no further soaking to be done. To try to do both on the same day might tempt you to work with damp stamps and this could damage them.

The next sorting step is to separate the foreign stamps from the U.S. issues. Put the foreign stamps aside for processing later. Remove any badly damaged stamps of either variety and discard them, as they only will cheapen your collection if they are retained. The only time a damaged stamp is worth saving is when it is a valuable issue and you are not likely to get a better copy in the near future. In such cases, put the stamp aside to save but make note of the fact that it is damaged and should be so marked when you put it in your album.

Catalogs and albums will separate U.S. stamps according to the service they were designed to render, so this is a good procedure to follow at this point in your sorting. Air-mail stamps are clearly marked and should be put in a separate pile. The same is true of special delivery, postage due and revenue stamps. Once these are screened out you are left with the regular and commemorative issues as described in the Introduction.

Take the commemoratives and separate them by face value. They are easy to spot as they usually are larger and fancier than the regular issues. Put all the five-centers together, all of the fours, all of the threes, and so on, up and down the price ladder. The lowest values should be placed in the pile starting at your left since they probably are the oldest stamps.

The regular issues should be kept in another group and should also be separated by denominations, the five-centers with the five-centers, the sixes with the sixes, and on up through the five-dollar issues.

For the time being, do not worry about duplication; simply put all the copies of each denomination together. The air-mails should be separated in the same manner and stacked from the lowest to the highest denominations.

Continue the procedures through the special deliveries, the postage dues, and any other categories you may have developed.

Building a Collection

Stamp packets such as these offer an easy way to begin your collection. Always buy the biggest packet you can afford as it will give you the widest assortment.

Your unused stamps can be separated in the same way as that described for the used stamps.

When you reach this point, you are ready to buy your first philatelic accessories. At a stamp store or philatelic counter buy several packages of glassines and a small stock book or a few stock-book pages. The glassines come in packages of a hundred. They are transparent envelopes which come in many sizes. Get about two hundred each of two or three sizes. The stock book is a book of pages which have many pockets designed to hold stamps. The more elaborate ones have interleaving between the pages; the simpler ones offer only the pockets. Single pages, punched to fit a three-ring binder, are also available. They probably are the most practical for the novice at this stage since they can be moved around in the binder as your collection grows. Be aware that you are going to pay extra for the binder if it has pictures of stamps on it or a fancy cover. An old used school binder can do the job just as well and the money saved can be used to buy stamps.

You have already sorted the commemoratives by variety, with all the duplicates together. Select from each pile the best copy you can find, one that is lightly canceled, nicely centered and undamaged, and put it in the stock book for transfer to your album when you reach that point in your collecting. Put all other copies in one of the glassine envelopes and set them aside for swapping purposes later.

When putting stamps in the stock book put them in the order established earlier—that is, from the lowest to the highest face value. Follow the same procedure with the regular issues and the specialized issues such as air-mails and postage dues. Using this system puts the stamps in the approximate sequence they will follow in the album. This will make the transfer from stock book to album easier when the time comes.

The sorting of your foreign stamps requires a somewhat different procedure, since you have a wider area to cover. Begin by separating the stamps by country. It will be easiest if you start with the English-speaking countries since their stamps are readily identifiable. Most countries, except Great Britain, put the name of the country on the stamp. All British stamps carry a portrait of the reigning monarch, so they, too, are easy to identify.

When you get beyond the English-speaking countries, the sorting gets trickier. This is particularly true when you begin to work with the stamps of those countries which use an alphabet different from the one with which we are familiar.

First put all of the stamps you can't identify into an envelope and label it your "mystery" envelope. It will be easy enough to get help with them later on. For now, concentrate on those foreign-language stamps you can identify without too much difficulty. *Polska,* for instance, tells you a stamp comes from Poland; *España* is Spain and *Italia* is Italy.

Other countries' markings will become familiar to you as you see them repeated in stamps in your accumulation. You soon learn that *Helvetia* is another name for Switzerland and *Suomi* is Finland. *Magyar Post* appears on the stamps of Hungary, and *Deutsche Bundespost* on the stamps of West Germany. Even if you can't identify the country from which the stamps come, sort them by common markings such as those listed above. This will make it easier to identify them as a group later. Foreign air-mails are fairly easy to spot as they usually carry words like *aero* or *avion* on them.

One foreign category which may puzzle new collectors is the semipostal since there is no equivalent United States category. These stamps carry two denominations on the face. For instance, a stamp of New Zealand could be marked "1¢ Health 3¢ Postage." The three cents pays for the postage; the extra penny is added to help pay for health programs. Many foreign countries use semipostals in one form or another; the money raised is often used to help youth programs.

After the preliminary sorting is completed, put all the stamps from one country in one envelope. Separate one good copy of each stamp and put it in the stock book for later

Semi-Postal Stamps

Some foreign nations issue stamps with an added charge which is used to support charitable organizations. This set from West Germany (Berlin) shows the charge added to each stamp.

mounting in an album. Use one or more stock-book pages for each country, depending on the number of stamps you have from each. Line the pages up alphabetically by country. Odd stamps can be bunched on a single page at the end of the book.

You now are beginning to get the first indication of the kinds of stamps which are going to be most readily available to you. From this you can decide the types you want to collect.

There are many choices: mint or used, U.S. or foreign, blocks or singles. Some collectors like the stamps of one country or one area, such as France and Colonies or Germany and Colonies. Others prefer to collect stamps from all over the world. Some want only unused stamps, others only used, still others a combination of many kinds. There is no "right" kind to collect. That is part of the fun of collecting, the freedom to choose what you want to save.

By now you probably have many duplicates. You will want to swap them with other collectors in order to get the stamps you need. There are several steps which should be taken before you do any major trading.

Stamp collectors tend to pile their extra stamps in boxes. This is not a practical way to keep stamps as it does not give any indication of what you have, what you can trade or what you might want to sell or give away.

Some type of check list will be helpful at this point. Many stamp dealers have printed price lists, which are usually free or inexpensive. They make excellent starters for knowing what you have and what you need. Take the stamps you have in your stock book and find them in the price list. Then put a check mark beside the number of each stamp you have. Later, when you go to stamp club meetings or stamp auctions, you can take your marked price list along and you will be able to tell at a glance whether you want or need a stamp which is being offered for sale or trade.

You will need a familiarity with stamp catalogs. Since they are discussed in Chapter Five, we will not go into details here other than to say that catalogs give you an introduction to comparing the value of one stamp with another. This makes it possible to swap stamps without any cash changing hands. There are, however, other considerations besides the catalog value which must be taken into account. These are discussed in detail in Chapter Five.

Where you have many stamps of one kind, gather them

into groups and put them in one of the glassine envelopes. They can be grouped according to denomination, with all of the four-centers in one envelope, the five-centers in another, and so on. They can be grouped according to use, that is, the air-mails with the air-mails, the special deliveries with the specials, and the commemoratives with the commemoratives. Where you have a quantity of one stamp, they should have a separate envelope. When you get familiar with catalog numbers you can mark the number on the outside of the envelope.

Sorting and processing stamps takes time. It is a job you never really finish since you are constantly adding to your collection. Keep it a fun part of the hobby. Do this by working with only small batches of stamps at a time. When it stops being fun and starts being work it is time to set aside the stamps for a few days.

Move slowly in collecting. If you take time to do each step right the first time, it won't have to be done over.

You now are ready to think about getting an album. How to make the best selection is the subject of the next chapter.

3
Picking an Album

Picking the right album is one of the important decisions you will be called upon to make in stamp collecting. The wrong choice could leave you with an album that has many pages you cannot fill, or it could leave you with many stamps for which no space has been provided. The best solution is to take a close look at the sorting you have just completed and determine your habits and wishes as a collector. Then you can find an album which best fits your collecting patterns.

For instance, if you are going to collect U.S. stamps, you will have to decide how deeply involved you want to get. If you are going to limit your collection to recent commemorative and regular issues, then you have little need for an album which allows space for envelopes, postal cards, revenue stamps, postage dues, and the many others specialized varieties.

Once you decide on the kind of collecting you are going to do, buy the best possible album you can afford. Mounting your stamp collection for the first time is a big job. If you use an album which is too small for your needs, then you will have to do the job all over again when you switch to a larger album.

The cheapest albums are the bound ones. These look like regular books but are permanently bound. The better albums are of the loose-leaf variety with removable pages. This makes it possible for you to add new pages each year. There is an added advantage. Not only can you add new pages, but you can remove the pages you do not want to use or you can insert blank pages for the areas from which you have many stamps.

Here's a good way to go about deciding on the kind of album you ought to buy. First, decide that you are going to collect stamps, not albums. This means that most of your spending should be on stamps rather than on the many extras which are peddled to stamp collectors. Beginners especially tend to buy all sorts of labels and stickers to put in their albums. This is wasteful because it doesn't add anything to the value of your collection and it uses up money which could be spent on stamps. It's also the mark of an amateur and you should graduate from this group as soon as possible.

If your collection is going to be mainly of stamps of the United States, then you should get a U.S. album and keep stamps from other areas in a stock book. If you are going to have only foreign stamps, then you will want a general foreign album. World-wide albums usually provide at least a few pages for U.S. stamps, but there are never enough if your United States collection is going to be growing at all.

If your collection is such that you have used only about half a dozen envelopes in the sorting, you probably will need a specialized album. If you have filled many envelopes, then you have the makings of a general collection and probably will need a world-wide album.

Back in the days when Great Britain headed an empire, there were albums for the stamps of Great Britain and her colonies. Now that most of the former colonies are independent, their stamps are in albums devoted to their part of the world. The stamps of Europe and Asia are most popular among foreign issues, so there is a wider choice of albums for them. There are, however, albums for stamps of most areas of the world, and there are individual albums for many of the more popular countries, like Italy, France and Germany, with their colonies.

Once you have decided on the area you are going to collect, visit one or more stamp stores and look over the album stock before making your final decision. Some of the bigger stores will have many kinds of albums on display. It is a good idea to buy your albums from a stamp dealer, or at least from a store which has a stamp department. A store which carries just a couple of albums on a table in a corner is not likely to be concerned about whether it can provide you with a supplement when you come back next year, nor will it always have the most up-to-date editions. If you live in a small town your stamp dealer may not carry albums, only folders telling about them. Almost any stamp dealer will be glad to mail you de-

Special Pages

Albums can be dressed up by the inclusion of special pages such as this one saluting U.S. accomplishments in space.

scriptive material about the albums he can order for you.

Talk to other collectors and ask about their albums. Find out what they like or dislike about the albums they are using. Their experience could save you from picking the wrong album.

A good basic album will have about two hundred pages and provide spaces for twenty-five thousand stamps. You should probably stick to one of the best-known brands when you pick an album. Scott, White Ace, Harris, Minkus are among the big names. One important reason for buying an album made by one of the larger companies is that you will be able to buy supplements to handle new issues each year. An album made by one of the smaller companies may or may not have annual supplements.

A few years back, the stamp album manufacturers put out new albums each year. Now they put out a basic album and update it with supplements for a few years before putting out a new edition. This means that when you buy your album you may also need to buy a few supplements to bring it up to date. These supplements cost a few dollars each, with the price varying according to the number of stamps issued during the year.

About a hundred years ago an album with spaces for all of the stamps issued throughout the world had only a few pages. A recent Scott's International Album consisted of seven volumes. It had more than 8,000 pages and spaces for about 175,000 stamps. The period covered was from 1840 through 1971. Each year about 5,000 to 8,000 new stamps are produced around the world.

The growth of new stamps is getting even faster as the former colonies become independent. Whenever a new country is formed, it changes its stamps and many new issues are added. In some areas, like the Middle East, countries move in and out of many alliances. Each time there is such a move the stamps of the countries involved are changed. It is a problem for the album maker to decide where to provide spaces for the new issues. It is also a problem for the collector to try and keep up with the answers found by the album manufacturers.

The newest thing in albums is the use of pages which have plastic pockets in them. The collector just drops the stamps into the pockets. This is a handsome way to display them and it does away with the danger of someone putting a finger mark on your prize stamp, but collecting in this fashion is very expensive. An album for a big country could cost more than one hundred dollars. Unless your stamps are extremely valuable, or you have a great deal of money, this kind of album should be left for the advanced collectors.

There are many ways in which to mount stamps in your album. The easiest way is through the use of hinges. These are made from paper which looks waxed but isn't. They are gummed on one side, just like your stamps. The gummed part of the hinge is moistened and then a part of it is applied to the back of the stamp. The rest of the hinge is stuck to the album page. When it dries the hinge will hold the stamp in place in the album. These hinges are specially designed so they can be removed without damaging the stamp. This makes it possible for you to move a stamp to another album at some time in the future, if you want.

Some notes of caution. Do not overmoisten the hinge. If you get it too wet, it will not hold the stamp. If the stamp is an unused one, the excess dampness could cause the stamp to stick to the page instead of just to the hinge. Don't attempt to remove a hinge while it is still damp. This will damage the stamp. Wait until the hinge is thoroughly dry.

Never use any other means of attaching the stamp to the page. Beginning collectors have destroyed valuable stamps by using tape, glue or other methods of pasting them down.

Hinges come two ways, flat and pre-folded. Both are good. The choice is up to the individual. Remember that the side that shines is the glue side, which is moistened when it is applied to the stamp.

There are other kinds of mounts which offer more protection for the stamps but cost considerably more than hinges. These are plastic and are gummed on the backs. The stamp is slipped inside the plastic and the mount is then stuck to the album page. Some of these mounts come cut to fit individual stamps, others come in strips that can be cut to the desired size.

How much you will want to spend on mounts depends on the size of your budget, the value of your stamps, and the amount of handling they will be getting. If your stamps are valuable, or if they are going to be handled a great deal, you may want to invest the extra money in the more protective mounts. Otherwise, you might consider it a smarter approach to put your money into stamps instead of into the accessories which can come later.

Good album maintenance is important. A stamp album that is not cared for gets to look shabby. Good maintenance begins with care in mounting the stamps. Hinges which are too damp or not damp enough will come loose and the stamps will fall out. Some stamps, as noted earlier, are printed in soluble inks. If you get the hinge too wet on a stamp of this type the color will smear and smudge the album page in addition to damaging the stamp.

Be sure the stamps are put in straight, right side up, and centered in the allotted space. When there are many stamps on the page, or when there are stamps on facing pages, a sheet of interleaving should be inserted between the pages to keep the stamps from getting caught on each other and being pulled off the page. The interleaf is a kind of waxed paper that comes in sheets punched to fit the album. It is available from stamp shops and costs a few cents a sheet.

When turning the pages of the album, hold the page at the upper right hand corner and flip it carefully. Too fast a turn can tear a page or shake a stamp loose from the hinge.

Many of the better albums come with a slipcase, a kind of cardboard cover that fits over the album and keeps out the dust and dampness. If your album does not have such a cover, then a plastic cover can be used, or even a cardboard box if you can find one the right size.

No one album or set of pages is going to satisfy all the needs of a collector, particularly as the collection grows and

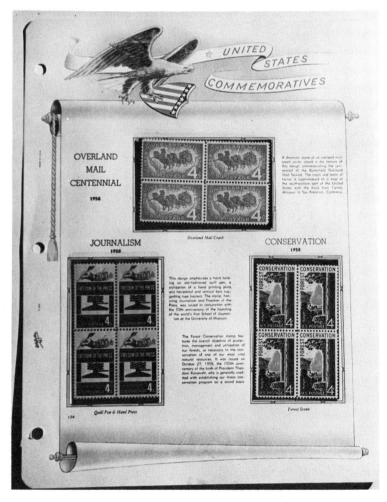

Giving the Stamp a Home

Stamp albums come in many shapes and sizes. This album is designed for blocks of United States stamps and provides a bit of history about each of the issues.

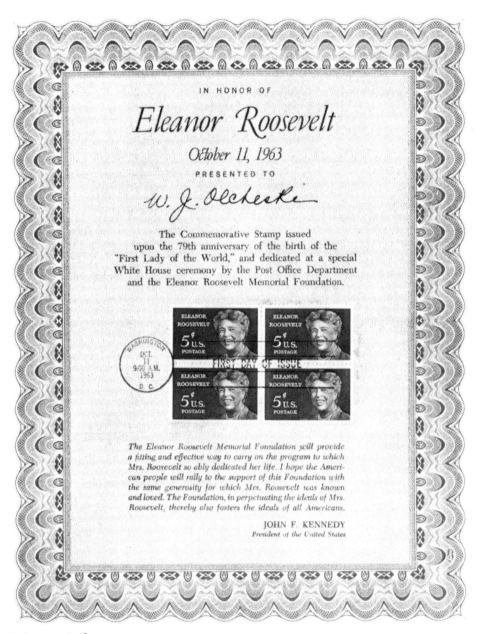

Salute to a Lady

The Eleanor Roosevelt
Memorial Foundation
produced this page as a
salute to Mrs. Roosevelt
at the time the stamp was
issued in her honor on
October 11, 1963.

interests change. There will be odd-sized stamps; some stamps you will want to keep on envelopes (or "on cover" as they are referred to by philatelists); and other special items. It is a good idea to consider creating your own album for this type of material.

Begin by buying a good three-ring binder. Blank pages may be purchased from a stationery store or stamp dealer. Get good heavy pages. They cost more but they hold up better. Pages can be bought with blank boxes drawn in for stamps, but with no other identification. Pages also may be purchased "quadrilled," that is, with finely crossed lines. The lines serve as a guide to placement of stamps on the page.

Blank pages give the collector a chance to put some of his or her personality into the collection. A Boy or Girl Scout might want to create a page for stamps which show Scouts. There are many such stamps. There is, in fact, a group which specializes in the collecting of stamps showing Scouts. On the same page with the Scout stamps the collector might want to put other items related to scouting. These could include merit badges, especially the one for stamp collecting; post cards canceled near the site of a camp-out; or anything else you might want to use to dress up the page.

Don't mount any stamps in your album until you are sure you know the proper place for each stamp. If you are not sure, check with a more experienced collector and get some advice. Many stamps look alike but are different because of watermarks, perforations or other distinguishing features. There could be a wide difference in the value of each type. The use of perforation gauges and watermark detectors will be explained in the next chapter.

If when mounting stamps, you come to one you cannot identify, put it in the "mystery" envelope you set aside earlier. When your envelope has about a dozen stamps in it, stop by a stamp store or talk to a more experienced collector and get held in finding out where the stamps belong. Never depend on a guess. If you don't know any advanced collectors, check at your library. The librarian can show you some books that will give clues to stamp identification. She also probably can put you in touch with a collector who can help you. If your area has a stamp club you undoubtedly can find help there. We will talk about clubs in Chapter Ten.

4

Stamp Talk

We have talked about the importance of getting the right stamp in the right place in your album. In order to be able to do this, you need to understand some of the basic terms in the language of philately.

The Postal Service produces stamps in several forms, according to the way they will be sold to the public. Each of these forms requires a separate place in your album.

When U.S. stamps are produced at the Bureau of Engraving and Printing in Washington, they are generally printed in sheets. These sheets break down into panes. The panes are what you really get when you go to the post office and ask for a sheet of stamps. The stamps on the pane are separated by punched holes which are called perforations. These holes go around all sides of the stamp.

Stamps of the same design in the regular series frequently are produced for sale in vending machines. These stamps are packaged in rolls or coils rather than in sheets or panes. The perforations are used primarily to feed the coils through the vending machine, so they generally appear on only the sides or the top and bottom of each stamp.

The same stamp design also may be produced for sale in booklets. Generally about six stamps are printed on a page and several of the pages are stapled within a cover to make up the booklet. Each such page is known as a booklet pane. The machine used to slice the booklets apart in the production process usually chops the perforations off at least one side of the stamps. If you find a single stamp with perforations on three sides, chances are good it came from a booklet pane.

Some early U.S. issues were released without any perforations. The purchaser had to use scissors to cut the stamps apart. Such stamps are known as imperforates. They often are found with uneven edges since the users were not concerned about keeping the stamps in good condition for collectors.

Tools of the Trade
These items are essential for proper stamp handling and identification: perforation gauges, stamp tongs, hinges, a watermark tray and a magnifying glass.

Revalued

When postal rates change the Postal Service sometimes revalues the envelopes it has in stock to make them conform to the new cost of sending a letter. This is done by printing an additional price alongside the existing stamp.

Two stamps which have the perforations around all the edges still could belong in different spaces in your album, sometimes many pages apart. This could occur because of differences in perforations. The stamps may have been produced at different times or perforated on different machines. The only way to tell them apart is through the use of a perforation gauge. This is an inexpensive plate, of metal, plastic or paper, which makes it possible to measure the perforations along the edges of a stamp. Often the difference is so minor that only an expert could identify the variation without using a perforation gauge.

Many U.S. stamps are perforated 11 x 10½. This does not mean that there are eleven holes across the top of the stamp. It means there are eleven perforations in the space of twenty millimeters, about $^{13}/_{16}$ of an inch.

Perforations are measured by sliding the stamp up and down the scale of the perforation gauge until the black dots on the gauge fit exactly into the holes at the edges of the stamp. Perforations are always measured across the top and down the sides of the stamp.

The use of such gauges becomes particularly important when you are dealing with U.S. stamps of the 1900–1930 period. Here you could have eight or more varieties of one stamp, all of them with a different value and with different places for them in your album, even though they look very much alike. A perforation gauge is a necessary investment if you are going to have stamps of this period in your collection. Some price lists produced for stamp dealers have a perforation gauge printed on the back cover. This type of gauge works perfectly well and there is no need to go out and buy another one unless you just want to have it to carry around in your pocket.

To understand how and why variations occur, let's look at two U.S. stamp issues. In 1929 the United States decided to put out a stamp for the fiftieth anniversary of the invention of the incandescent lamp by Thomas A. Edison. The stamps were designed for issue in sheets, with printing on flat-bed presses; those scheduled to be released in coils were to be printed on rotary presses.

What the Postal Service didn't count on was the great interest the stamp would create among firms involved in the production of electricity and electronic products. When the demand became very heavy, the Postal Service produced the stamps as fast as it could by whatever means it had available, including stamps printed on a rotary press, in sheets as well as in coils. As a result, we have three varieties, and three separate places for them in the album. One way of telling them apart is by measuring the perforations. The flat-plate printing is perforated 11; the rotary-press printing is perforated 11 x 10½; and the rotary-press coil stamp is perforated 10 vertically.

When the stamps were produced there were different numbers of each type printed. Final figures showed 31 million of the flat plate variety; 210 million of the rotary-press sheet type; and 133 million of the coils. This uneven distribution made some of the stamps harder to get than others. As a result, one type is worth almost six times as much as the other.

The Harding Memorial issue of 1923 was another example of a stamp which attracted a great deal of public interest and forced the Postal Service to take special steps to meet the demand. The stamp was issued in flat plate, rotary-press and imperforate printings. Here, too, the difference in value among the varieties is substantial.

In more recent years, paper shortages have resulted in the creation of postal card varieties. This happened because the available paper supply ran out before all the cards had been printed and a different grade of paper had to be substituted for the rest of the printing. The same thing happens occasionally on foreign stamps, causing variations and therefore the need for separate spaces in the album.

It is important to remember that the first business of the Postal Service is to carry the mail. The production of stamps is designed to make it possible to prepay for such services. Any number of circumstances, from paper shortages to unexpected demands, can cause the Postal Service to resort to a variety of production methods to meet the needs. This produces the many varieties which add interest, fun and challenge to collecting.

When a stamp appears in several forms the collector needs to be alert not only to get the stamp in the right place in the album, but to be sure he or she has not been sold an altered stamp—that is, a cheap variety which has been changed to make it look like a more valuable stamp. Suppose, for instance, that an imperforate variety of a stamp is worth more than the same design stamp with perforations all around. The unwary collector could end up buying a regular stamp from which the perforations had been trimmed. The best safeguard against this is to place the stamp you believe to be an imperforate on top of a perforated stamp of the same design. If the perforations have been cut off, the supposed imperforate stamp will be smaller and you can readily tell it is homemade and should be discarded as merely a damaged stamp.

When paper was produced many centuries ago, the process involved boiling old rags and other materials along with some chemicals and then drying the resulting pulp into crude sheets. This drying was done by pouring the liquid pulp into rough frames. As the pulp dried, the frames left faint markings in the paper which had been produced. These "watermarks" often served to identify the maker of the paper.

In stamp production, watermarked paper, with special watermark designs, was often used as a means of preventing counterfeiting. While the creator of fake stamps might be able to match the design, it was thought unlikely that he could also match the watermarked paper. This use for watermarks has lessened, but many countries still use watermarked paper for printing their stamps.

On stamps of some European countries the watermarks are visible to the naked eye. Pick up a stamp of Great Britain and look at the back. It often is possible to spot a crown or portion of a crown in the gum. Watermarks on U.S. stamps are a bit more elusive. Their importance for our purpose is limited to the fact that they may be the only means of telling two stamps apart when the designs are identical.

There is an inexpensive method for finding out if a U.S. stamp is watermarked. You need a black glass or plastic tray and some watermark fluid. This fluid can be purchased from a stamp dealer. To determine if a stamp is watermarked, place it face down in the tray. Add a few drops of watermark fluid. If there is a watermark, it will pop right out and show its design. As soon as you have decided if there is a watermark, use your tongs to remove the stamp from the tray. The fluid will evaporate, the watermark will disappear and the stamp will appear as before.

A few words of warning about working with watermark fluid. Do not work in a closed space as the fumes can make you sick. Keep the top on the bottle at all times when not pouring the fluid. It evaporates very rapidly and your supply will disappear if the bottle is left open. Do not use too much fluid; a few drops are enough. If you use too much or leave the stamp in it too long, it could cause the colors to fade. Finally, do not allow anyone to smoke near you while you are working with the fluid. It is highly inflammable.

Amateur collectors sometimes look for substitutes for watermark detector fluid. This is unwise. Lighter fluid, for instance, will cause the watermarks to appear, but it contains oil which could leave marks on the stamps.

The watermark on United States stamps in the 1895–1917 period generally consists of the initials U.S.P.S., for United States Postal Service. It appears in single or double line letters. Not all of the letters appear on any one stamp. They are printed across the back of the sheets. Therefore the stamp you have may show only a portion of one of the letters. But this usually is enough to tell you the group of stamps with which it belongs in your album. There is much technical detail about watermarks with which you need not concern yourself at this time. If, as you progress in the hobby, your interests turn to specialization in watermarks, there is plenty of literature on the subject.

Sometimes varieties of stamps are created unintentionally. This was what happened back in 1934 when the U.S. government decided to issue a series of stamps honoring the national parks. A set of ten stamps, ranging in value from one to ten cents, was prepared and issued as usual with perforations. A short time after the stamps went on sale the word got out that some sheets of the stamps had been distributed to certain government officials before the stamps had been perforated or the gum applied. The number of such stamps was very limited and the demand for them was high. Prices soared. The government bowed to collector protests, reprinted the stamps and distributed them without gum or perforations in addition to the regular form. That's why you will find two sets of spaces in your album for the National Parks stamps and several other stamps of the same period.

In 1962 the United States put out a stamp honoring Dag Hammarskjöld, secretary-general of the United Nations who died in a plane crash. The stamp showed the secretary-general and the U.N. Headquarters building in New York. Shortly after the stamp was issued, it was learned that some of the stamps had appeared with the yellow background inverted. This apparently was because some of the sheets had been turned the wrong way while being fed into the presses. There was no way of knowing how many stamps were affected. The Postal Service decided to print 40 million of the "error" stamps in order to satisfy collector demand. There were 121 million of the original stamps printed, but no one ever will know how many of them were errors. As a result of the reprinting, you have two spaces for Hammarskjöld stamps in your U.S. album. Specialized albums have even more space for this stamp since the appearance of the error differs on stamps from the middle of the pane and those on the rows at the end.

As mail volume increases, the postal services of the world are looking for ways to speed the sorting of mail. One device they use is an electronic eye screening which performs a variety of tasks. It can place the letters in proper position for canceling; it can separate air mail from regular mail; it can direct letters with certain markings into sorting bins for dispatch to various areas.

All of this is made possible by the placing of special "tagging" or marking on the stamps in phosphor. When these tagged stamps pass the electric eye, it reacts to the chemicals and causes the letters to be sorted into the desired categories. The application of this phosphor coating to some stamps and not to others means that the treated and untreated ones go in different spots in your album.

Normally the coating on the stamps is not visible without the use of detectors. On some British stamps, however, the coating can be spotted by tilting the stamp in the light. The bands of phosphor stand out when this is done.

There are several varieties of ultraviolet or black light detectors on the market to aid in identifying tagged stamps. These devices are expensive and need not be part of the equipment of the average stamp collector. Stamp dealers usually have one or more in their shops and ordinarily will be willing to check a few stamps for you and let you know if they are tagged.

Pre-Cancels

Business firms which mail in quantity often use pre-canceled stamps since they go through the postal service without need for further processing. The name of the city is stamped across the front of the stamp. Business users need a special permit to be able to use stamps of this type.

A note of caution. The "black lights" used to make posters glow in the dark normally will not work in bringing out the phosphor markings on stamps.

In sorting your U.S. issues, you probably will come across some stamps with the name of a city printed on them, usually with a line over and under the city name. This variety is known as a precancel. As the name suggests, the stamps are canceled prior to use. They are intended for business firms or other large mailers who will be sending thousands of envelopes of the same size and weight at the same time, such as in the mailing of an advertising circular. Use of the precanceled stamps means the letters can move through the post office without being delayed by the cancellation process. One of the earliest uses of this type of cancellation was at Cumberland, Maine, in 1857. Today there are several thousand variations of such cancels.

A stamp of this type can be put in your album in the space marked for the particular stamp, even though it has the city name on it. There is a whole area of collecting precancels. Normally precancel collectors are interested only in the city name and do not care on which stamp it appears. This makes it hard to swap stamps with them since the same precancel might appear on a cheap stamp or an expensive one.

Another variety of stamp you may run across in your sorting is one which has holes punched through it, usually in the form of initials. These can be found in stamps issued as far back as 1907. Large business houses punched the initials of the company name into the stamps to keep their employees from stealing the stamps and reselling them. To a lesser degree the use of initials was designed to keep the employees from using the stamps on their personal mail. It was easy for a mail clerk to spot an outgoing letter with a stamp which had the company initials in it and thus know that the stamp had been taken from company stock.

The many varieties of perforated initials gave rise to the collecting of this type of stamp, which is called a "perfin." The initials appear on both U.S. and foreign stamps. Collectors of this variety, like the precancel collectors, are interested in the initials rather than the stamp, so swaps with them can be difficult. Perforated initial collectors often mount the stamps face down on black pages in their albums so the initials can be seen more clearly.

If your collection includes early United States issues, you are likely to run across grill stamps of 1867–71. These are stamps in which a series of tiny depressions or pits have been made by a roller. They were designed so that the ink used in the cancellation of the stamp ran into these pits, thus making it impossible for Postal Service customers to wash off the cancellations and use the stamps over again. Grilled stamps are easy to spot just by looking at the backs where the miniature waffle pattern is usually clearly visible. There are variations within the grills, but you will need experienced help in separating them at this time.

There are many other variations of stamps you will run across in your collecting. We have attempted here to discuss only a few most likely to be encountered by a beginner.

Catalogs will be a great aid to you as your collecting advances. In the next chapter we will talk about catalogs, what they are and how you use them to further your understanding and enjoyment of the hobby.

5
Catalogs

Catalogs play an important part in the philatelic world. They provide a means of stamp identification for collectors, which can be used in buying, selling or trading.

A catalog number is assigned to every stamp issued in the world. It is this number which is used to identify the stamps in the album, in stamp advertisements, in price lists and in most writing about philatelic matters.

There are two major systems of catalog numbers used in the United States. The oldest, and by far the most widely used, is that produced by the makers of Scott catalogs and other philatelic products. Of more recent vintage are the Minkus numbers. These are used chiefly in albums and other stamp publications produced for sale through outlets in major department stores around the country. For the most part, Scott numbers are used on price lists and in advertising by the majority of stamp companies. The comparative advantages of the different numbering systems will be discussed later in this chapter.

Once governments began issuing stamps and people began to collect them, it was inevitable that some means be devised for keeping the stamps in order. This led to the creation of stamp catalogs.

On the letterhead of the Scott Publishing Company is the legend "The People Who Invented Stamp Collecting." They have a reasonable claim to the title. It was back in 1863 that John Walter Scott began dabbling in stamps and it was in 1867 that his first "stamp catalogue" came into being.

Before we get into how and why you use a catalog, let's take a brief look at the history of the Scott organization and how the imagination and ingenuity of one man helped give some semblance of order to a hobby that captures the interest of millions of people around the world.

George T. Turner, writing in the October 1967 issue of *Scott's Monthly Journal*, tells us something of the early life of Scott and of the development of his "catalogue."

Scott was born in England in 1843 and began collecting stamps when he was about eleven years old. One day, when he was almost seventeen, he watched a bearded man pay a British pound for four American stamps. Scott was astounded that such a large sum of money could be obtained for a few stamps. On the spot he decided to become a stamp dealer.

The next year he moved to the United States. The first thing he did after arriving in New York was to run out of money. The quickest way he could think of to raise funds was to sell some of his stamp collection. He sold the stamps to William P. Brown, a stamp and coin dealer. Brown's business was new and growing and he saw great prospects for philately in America. He persuaded Scott to enter the stamp business and made him a loan of a hundred dollars' worth of his stock to get him started. Scott was able to repay the loan within three months.

However, he wasn't making money fast enough in the stamp business, so he decided to go west and hunt for gold. When he didn't find any, he returned in 1867 to New York and the stamp business.

Scott put out his first catalog the same year, though it was actually nothing more than a price list of the stamps that he had available for sale. There had been "catalogs" earlier, but they were merely lists of stamps without any prices. They were printed and distributed by stamp dealers who then put out their own price lists to go along with them. Scott combined both the listings and the prices into his catalog.

The September 1868 Scott price list was probably the first real catalog. It had twenty-four pages and sold for fifteen cents. Scott also began production of albums the same year. The catalog grew slowly. By 1892 it had doubled to forty-eight pages and the price had increased to twenty-five cents. It was not until 1943 that the number of stamp issues had reached a level where it was necessary for the Scott Publishing Company to split the catalog into two volumes.

The Scott catalog now has grown to three volumes, with a fourth specialized volume covering only the issues of the United States. The cost of the entire set has increased to a point where it is both unnecessary and unwise to get a new set each year unless you plan to enter the stamp business on a professional basis. Your library probably has one or more catalogs, although they may be a few years old. Talk to the librarian and you may be able to get her to order the latest issue which would then be available for your use.

Early catalogs listed stamps of all the world, usually in alphabetical order, although the stamps of the United States appeared at the front of the book in some of them. From time to time there have been limitations on the use of illustrations of U.S. stamps in catalogs and albums. This was because of fear of counterfeiting. In recent years these rules have been liberalized, but for reasons of space many catalogs illustrate only one stamp of a set and then provide a description of other stamps in the series.

Catalogs may be frightening to the beginner. They are big and look as if they would be too complicated to understand. However, this is not the case. Early exploration of a catalog is a good step for a new collector. The best place to do this is the library.

Let's look at how a catalog can be used to show you where a certain stamp goes in your album. At the same time we can become familiar with the other kinds of information you can find in a catalog. Since this book deals primarily with the collecting of United States stamps, we will limit our discussion to the two leading U.S. catalogs, the *Scott United States Stamp Catalogue, Specialized* and the *New American Stamp Catalog* produced by Minkus Publications.

In order to find where to put a stamp in the album we have to know the date, at least the year, in which it was issued. The catalog is the place to go for this kind of information.

The stamps are listed in chronological order, with the

oldest stamps in the front of the book and the newer issues toward the back. Scott separates the issues into regular and air-mail issues with separate listings for each. The regular and commemorative stamps are listed first and numbered in sequence. The air-mail stamps, listed separately, also are numbered in sequence, but there is a *C* in front of the number for an air-mail stamp. Thus, the first regular stamp is numbered *1* while the first air-mail stamp is numbered *C-1*.

The Minkus system uses a regular numerical sequence for definitive or regular issues. Catalog numbers for commemoratives are preceded by *CM* and those for air-mail issues by an *A*.

There is no way to match systematically the Scott and Minkus numbers because of the different arrangement methods in the catalogs.

Suppose in your collecting you come across the U.S. stamp showing Walt Disney, the creator of Mickey Mouse. You will want to find where it goes in your album and you are going to turn to the Scott catalog for help. First you examine the stamp and look for clues to when it was issued. There is no date on the stamp, so that easy solution is ruled out. Now the search begins.

Stamps in the catalog are arranged chronologically—that is, in the order of the time at which they came out. U.S. stamps are not issued to honor living persons. Since Walt Disney was alive not too many years ago, it is obvious that we will not look for his stamp in the early pages of the catalog. Our next clue comes in the face value of the stamp. We see this is a six-cent stamp. Postage rates for the most part have increased regularly through the years. We therefore have a sequence of three-cent, four-cent, five-cent commemorative stamps and so on, reflecting the rate changes over the years.

Now all we have to do is look in the catalog for the grouping of six-cent commemoratives. The picture is easy to spot in the catalog and we learn that the Disney stamp was issued in 1968. We find that the Scott catalog number is 1355. If your album is a Scott album, all you need do is turn to the page with a space for 1355 and you have the right spot for your stamp. If your album is other than Scott, turn to the pages for the commemorative stamps of 1968 and you will find a place for the Disney issue.

The catalog tells us considerably more than the place to put the stamp in the album. For the Disney stamp, for instance, it tells us the date of issue, September 11, 1968; the name of the designer, C. Robert Moore; and the manner in which it was issued, eight panes of fifty stamps on a plate of four hundred stamps. You will remember that what we call a sheet of stamps at the post office is actually one of those eight panes which make up the printed sheet (page 32).

The catalog tells us the number of perforations—twelve; that the stamp is tagged,—that is, coated with a phosphorescent material for use in mechanical letter sorting; and that it has no watermark.

It gives us the catalog price for the stamp in a number of different forms. The stamp is priced used and unused as a single stamp. In the U.S. Specialized Catalog it is also priced used and unused as a block of four. Often this is merely four times the price of a single stamp, but there are important exceptions, particularly if there is more than one design on a single pane of stamps. The block then could be worth many times the price of the four single stamps.

We are given a price for a plate block, a Mr. ZIP block and a Mail Early block. We also learn of errors or variations which make the stamp of special interest or value. For instance, there is a variety of the Walt Disney stamp which is missing the dark yellow color. Other varieties are missing the black or the blue color. The catalog tells us that horizontal pairs of these stamps are known to exist without perforations between the stamps.

The Minkus catalog takes a little different approach in that it provides more general information about each of the stamps and uses a slightly different method of pricing. The handling of the stamp honoring the newspaper boys of America is a good illustration of the approach used.

To find a stamp in the Minkus catalog you would use the same procedure as outlined for the Scott catalog, but you would have to keep in mind that this is a commemorative stamp and so will be in the commemorative section.

Minkus assigns the stamp a number (CM 357). He tells us the stamp came out in 1952 and then tells why it was released. "The Newspaper Boys of America issue recognized the service of America's newsboys and the value of their early business training. It also complimented the meeting of the International Circulation Managers Association held at Philadelphia in October of 1952."

We are told this is a three-cent stamp, violet in color. The issue date of October 4 is shown and the total number of stamps printed (115,430,000) is listed. As in the Scott catalog, the stamp is priced both mint and used. It is priced as a single, a block of four, a plate block, and a sheet of fifty stamps. An added feature is the listing of a price for a first-day cover.

Each of the catalogs provides specialized information and background not only about stamps but about envelopes, revenue stamps, postal cards and other special issues. The Scott catalog provides an alphabetical index of all U.S. commemorative stamps, making it easy to find the catalog number simply by looking up the subject in the alphabetical list.

Regular issues are a bit harder to find in the catalog. A new series comes out every few years. There was a series running from one cent to five dollars in 1901. Many of the regular issues you get in your early collecting will be from the 1922–25 series. Regular stamps in the Presidential series were issued in 1938. The Liberty issue covered the period 1954 through 1968. The Prominent Americans series ran from 1965 to 1973. The persons illustrated will give a clue to the time of issue. Beyond that, you just have to make a good guess and then check one of the lists mentioned in this paragraph.

The greatest value of a catalog is to identify a stamp and give you a basis for keeping your stamps in some kind of order. You shouldn't rely on the catalog as a price list. Don't confuse catalog price with selling price, or even with value; there is a big difference. The catalog has only one price for a stamp, regardless of condition. Yet a stamp which is in perfect condition may be worth much more than the listed price, while one that is slightly damaged or heavily canceled may be worth much less.

Stamps often are sold at a percentage of catalog price. The trouble with this is that the percentage varies from one country to another. A stamp from a country which is very popular with collectors may sell at or even above the catalog price. A stamp from a country in which there is little interest may sell for only a small fraction of the catalog price.

The catalogs are not an exact guide to price even for trading purposes. A collection of one hundred stamps which catalog three cents each is not a fair trade for one stamp which catalogs three dollars, even though the "book" value seems to be the same. This is because the minimum catalog price on a stamp in 1975 was three cents, no matter how common the stamp. A collection of one hundred of the most common varieties of stamps would catalog three dollars, but actually would be worth closer to fifty cents.

Some European catalog publishers are also stamp dealers and their catalogs are in effect price lists for their stamps. These are a much more reliable indicator of what it would cost to replace the stamps you have or to add to your collection.

Some U.S. firms, like H. E. Harris of Boston, put out an annual catalog which uses Scott numbers. This is really a price list and must be considered separately from the catalogs.

A used catalog can be of almost as much value to you as a new one. The information, other than price, does not change on the older stamps each year. An old catalog is an excellent place to keep track of your stamp inventory. A small check mark in the catalog lets you know the stamps you have, whether they are mint or used, singles or blocks, plate blocks or first-day covers. A quick run through such a check list shows you what you have and what you need, what extras you have and what you can trade.

Another thing a catalog does is tell you if a stamp is a single or part of a set. If it is part of a set, the catalog gives you at least a list of the other stamps in the set, even if it doesn't illustrate all of them. Look also for footnotes in the catalog listings which will tell you if other stamps were added to the set in later years. This is particularly true of regular issues which are designed for long-term use. A rate change, for instance, creates the need for a stamp of a new denomination. The new stamp is issued and numbered into the regular series which may have been released a few years earlier. When a regular definitive series is issued, spaces occasionally are left in the numbering sequence to allow for the insertion of additions at a later date.

This was what happened in the regular issue series of 1970–73. Look at Scott Numbers 1397 through 1400, covering stamps which you would expect to have been issued at the same time. In fact, they were not. Scott Number 1397 is the fourteen-cent stamp showing Fiorello H. LaGuardia. It was issued April 24, 1972. Number 1398 is the sixteen-cent stamp showing Ernie Pyle. It was issued May 7, 1971. Number 1399 was not used and Number 1400 is the twenty-one cent stamp showing Amadeo P. Giannini. It was issued June 27, 1973. The issue dates span a number of years, but the stamps would go in sequence on the same page in your album.

Look on the catalog as a guidebook and locator rather than as an effective price list and you will have learned how to use one more tool which can add pleasure and progress to your collecting activities.

6
Special Kinds of Collecting

It is not long after you start down the highway of collecting that you realize it has many interesting detours. Trips down these byways add interest to the hobby and need not distract you from collecting in the traditional ways.

One of the most interesting of these special areas is the field of topical collecting. As the name suggests, this means the accumulation of stamps featuring designs which deal with some particular topic. Some topics are very broad, such as animals on stamps. Others may be much more limited, such as bicycles.

Topical and other specialized forms of collecting are often a natural by-product of your regular collecting. You buy a box or packet of stamps and take out the stamps you need in your regular collection. Now you take a second look at what is left. Among the U.S. issues you have some with the names of cities printed on the face of them. These are the precancels described earlier. A few of them mounted on a page make an interesting addition to your collection.

A Fun Touch

Local Post issues add a fun touch to collecting. They are not valid for postage. The cost of the stamps covers the cost of delivery of the mail from the residence of the mailer to the nearest mailbox. The owner of this "Local Post" used his Cadillac to make the delivery.

Topicals

Flowers on stamps are among the more popular topical items. These flowers are on a first day cover from Belgium.

Here in the corner of the box are a few stamps with initials punched through them. These are the perfins, carrying the identifying mark of the owner to prevent use of the stamps for postage by unauthorized persons. Mounted face up or down, they add spice to a collection. If there are foreign stamps in the group, you are bound to have openings for several topical collections. Look at them with an eye toward your special interests. If you like art, there are paintings and painters on stamps. If you lean toward more active pursuits, there are racing cars, planes, boats and all kinds of sports on stamps. If architecture interests you, there are thousands of stamps showing buildings. There even are pictures of stamps on stamps for the collector who wants to stay really close to the hobby.

The American Topical Association is made up of collectors who specialize in topical stamps. It has more than ten thousand members in some ninety countries. The association recently compiled a list of the most popular stamp topics among collectors. Animals rated at the top. This is understandable since it is such a broad category. Think of some of the possibilities you could have in your own collecting with this topic.

The second spot in the American Topical Association poll went to space on stamps. In this, as in any other topical collec-

Animals on Stamps

Australian wildlife is featured on this set of four stamps issued in 1974. Many countries issue stamps which show animals found in their area.

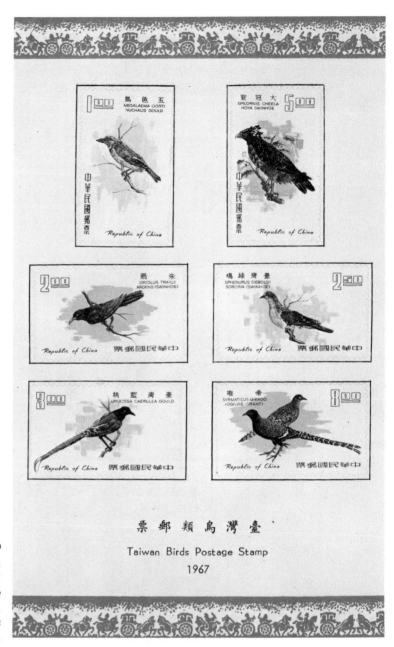

Collectors of birds on stamps were delighted with this set issued by the Republic of China in 1967. It featured birds native to Formosa.

tion, the collector usually includes both United States and foreign stamps. Thus a collection of space stamps could include varieties from many parts of the world.

A growing topical area, and third on the association list, is Americana. This category can be expected to grow as the ever-increasing number of bicentennial issues is made available to the public. In future years it is likely that entire albums will be devoted to stamps issued for the American bicentennial. It is also probable that stamps of this type will be popular with people outside the United States. If this proves true, the stamps will be harder to get and so will go up in value faster than other stamps issued during the same period.

Many foreign countries take advantage of the high interest in topical stamps among collectors in the United States. It is not unusual for foreign countries with no obvious interest in the United States to put out a series of stamps which they know will appeal to American collectors. In recent years we have seen quite a few stamps showing the late President John F. Kennedy issued by nations thousands of miles away on the Persian Gulf. Such stamps are often costly when they first appear, as their bright colors and flashy designs make them popular, particularly with new collectors. However, they often drop sharply in value as they are not highly regarded by the more seasoned collectors.

The area of paintings on stamps is another which is much exploited by some "stamp-happy" countries. The stamps of such nations are easy to spot. Usually they are extra large and colorful, and the stamps are priced higher than other recently issued stamps. Frequently, if purchased "used," the stamps of these countries are found to have their original gum on the back, even though they theoretically have been used to carry a

Popular Subject

Scouts on stamps are a popular subject for topical collectors. Here are a few scout stamp issues from around the world.

Scout Salute

Foreign countries provide many attractive covers as part of their salute to Boy and Girl Scout programs.

Pick and Choose

Approval dealers send mounted selections of stamps which the collector can buy and pay for or return to the dealer without making a purchase. This is a Scout set as offered by one such dealer.

letter. This happens because the stamps are canceled while they are still on the printing presses. These stamps are designed for sale to collectors and were never intended to be used. They are known as CTO. That means "canceled to order." They are easy to identify since the cancellation touches only the corner of each stamp. If you saw a block of four of the stamps, you would notice that the four cancellations together make up a circle about the size of a quarter. This makes the stamps attractive to collectors since the cancellation does not obscure the design. It also makes it possible for the stamps to be canceled four at a time with a minimum of effort.

If you are to be a serious collector of topicals, you probably will end up with some of these "wallpaper" issues in your collection. There is no harm in this, but you should know that the resale value on stamps of this type is negligible, should you decide to give up collecting and sell your stamps at some time in the future.

This is not to suggest that all bright and colorful stamps are cheap exploitations of the collector. There are many beautiful art stamps issued by such countries as France, Spain and Italy which are both attractive and legitimate.

Some topical subjects are so popular that you can buy special pages or even albums for them. For most of the others you will have to design your own pages, using blanks.

If you are in Boy or Girl Scouts, this is a whole area of topical collecting. Your album pages can include not only stamps which honor scouting programs, but could also contain merit badges, patches and other souvenirs of your scouting

Pienellä Shrub Oakin kaup... ...
Yhdysvalloissa on omalaatuinen yk-
sityinen postitoimisto, jonka pos-
teljoonina toimii Alfie, saksanpai-
menkoira. Koiraposti käyttää omaa
postimerkkiäänkin, joka tosin ei
kelpaa muualle menevin lähetyk-
siin, niihin on liimattava »oikeat»
postimerkit. Eräs asia on varma:
tätä »posteljoonia» ei koirien auta
tulla puraisemaan, Alfie voi purra
takaisin!

SHRUB OAK
LOCAL DOG POST
2c

SHRUB OAK
LOCAL DOG POST
2c

SHRUB OAK

Koirapostin 2 centin postimerkki

Mr. Herst, koirapostitoimiston
»johtaja», neuvottelee asioista »pos-
teljooni» Alfien kanssa.

Alfie valmiina viemään kirjeen »at-

World Famous

"Alfie" was known around the world as can be seen in this article in a foreign magazine. His owner, Herman Herst, is shown at the side, along with two of the "Local Post" stamps used by Herst on letters carried by Alfie.

activities. Such a collection makes a good display for a program at a Scout meeting.

A big drawback to topical collecting is that it does not group the stamps in any standard order. A collection of medicine on stamps concerns itself only with the medical subjects shown in the design. If the collection were to be broken up and put in regular albums, the sorting job would be a big one.

There is an answer to the problem. As you mount each stamp in its place, lightly pencil in under it the appropriate

Scott or Minkus catalog number. In this way you can readily identify the stamp if you want to move it to another album or if you want to make an inventory of the catalog value of your collection.

The limits placed on topical collecting, like the limits put on all types of stamp collecting, are up to the collector. Just for fun, let's wander down one of the detours on the collecting highway and take a look at the topical area of animals on stamps. To be more specific, let's look just at dogs on stamps. Topical collectors not only collect the stamps, but, as we have indicated earlier, stories and other items related to the topic. Here are short stories about three dogs involved with stamps. Each story could be the basis for a good page in your album.

We begin with Alfie. This is the story of a German shepherd dog who was assigned the job of delivering the mail in a little New York village called Shrub Oak. To say he delivered the mail is an exaggeration of his role, since the delivery of mail in the United States is a monopoly limited by law to the United States Postal Service, Actually, Alfie was supposed to carry the mail from his home to the nearest mailbox. His owner, Herman Herst, Jr., a well-known stamp writer, organized the "Shrub Oak Local Post" so that his children could play mailman and deliver letters from the homes of his neighbors to the mailbox at two cents per letter. He even produced stamps which the youngsters could affix to the letters. These, of course, had to be supplemented by regular postal issues to cover mailing cost once the letters got to the mailbox.

The youngsters soon got tired of the game, so Alfie was pressed into service. He delivered the letters from his master and two neighbors to the mailbox. Whoever went to the box with Alfie then took the letters and mailed them. Alfie's territory was limited, since he was not allowed to cross the street.

The story of Alfie was carried in many newspapers and eventually his fame spread overseas. The "local post" stamps issued by Herst for Alfie's mail service carried a picture of the dog. Copies of the stamps have found their way into many collections.

The United States Information Service told Alfie's story abroad and later mentioned that he had been injured in an accident. He got hundreds of sympathy cards. A German news magazine did a story about him and schoolchildren wrote to him, asking for one of the special stamps and an inked paw print. Herst says the demand was so heavy that Alfie still whimpers whenever he sees a stamp pad.

Owney,
Mascot of the
Railway Mail
Service

The Postal Dog

Owney, the Postal Dog, was featured in this pamphlet published by the Smithsonian Institution in Washington, D.C.

Alfie has gotten old now and moved into retirement with his master in Florida. Someday he may end up in a museum as an interesting sidelight in philatelic history.

Another famous postal dog already is in a museum. He is Owney, a dog who became a mascot of the Railway Mail Service late in the 1880s. The Division of Philately and Postal History of the Smithsonian Institution in Washington, where Owney rests in a display case, reports that over the years it has received more requests for information about Owney than about any other aspect of postal history.

Owney wandered into the Albany, New York, post office one cold day in 1888 and was befriended by the employees. He soon was riding atop the mail sacks on wagons which took the mail from the Albany Post Office to the local railway depot. The clerks allowed him to ride along as the mail was carried to distant cities. They put an Albany mail tag on his collar so he would be returned home if he got separated from his friends along the way. Before long, he was traveling to many cities and picking up many identification tags from the places he visited. They eventually covered a coat which was presented to him by Postmaster General John Wanamaker.

Carl Scheele, of the Smithsonian's Division of Philately and Postal History, reports that Owney's travels carried him to Paris, Kentucky; Charlestown, Massachusetts; Puyallup, Washington; Detroit, Michigan; Denver, Colorado; Philadelphia, Pennsylvania; Atlanta, Georgia; Brookings, South Dakota; Reno, Nevada; Cincinnati, Ohio; Manchester, New Hampshire; El Paso, Texas; Bald Knob, Arkansas; and Winnipeg, Canada. He hastens to add that this is only a partial list of the territory covered by Owney.

Postal workers in Tacoma, Washington, arranged for Owney to take a trip around the world, which he did beginning in August and ending in December of 1895. He covered 143,000 miles. When he died in 1897, postal clerks contributed funds to have him preserved by a taxidermist. He was transferred to the Smithsonian in 1911.

Dogs appear on the stamps of many countries of the world. Perhaps one of the most famous dogs is Laika, the space dog recognized as the first space traveler. The animal appears on two stamps released by Rumania on December 20 in 1957. The stamps show the dog and the Sputnik II spaceship.

Sometimes a stamp could fit into a number of different

Presidents

Four of the seven U.S. presidents who died in office were assassinated, Lincoln, Garfield, McKinley and Kennedy. Two of them, Lincoln and Kennedy, are shown on this combination first-day cover.

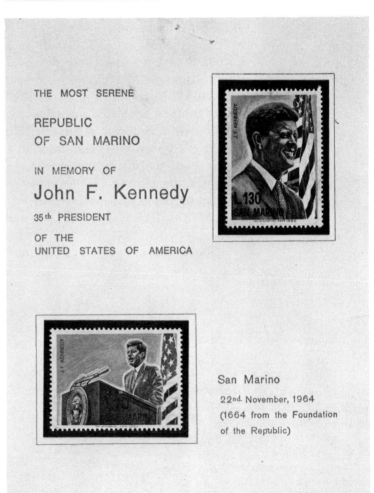

Souvenir Sheet

This souvenir sheet from far-off Ajman honors President Kennedy and his family.

Many Honors

Postal tributes to the Kennedys came from many nations far from the President's homeland. These stamps came from South Arabia.

Navy Covers

The launching of a ship and the observance of Navy Day provided two more covers for the collectors of Kennedy-related stamp items.

collections. Such is the case with the Laika dog stamp. This commemorative logically could be in a collection of dog stamps or a collection of space stamps.

There is almost no limit to the special area into which you can divert your collecting interests. First-day covers are discussed in detail in the next chapter. Postal stationery gets you into everything from postal cards to aerogrammes. Revenue stamp collecting is a whole field in itself with the many varieties of documentary and tax stamps.

Even if this kind of collecting doesn't appeal to you right now, it is good to keep it in mind for the day when you have built your regular collection to a point where additions to it are both costly and hard to acquire. That's when your special types of collecting give you a chance to continue in the hobby while staying within your budget.

Many of the special areas of collecting have large groups of followers. They are members of special groups and they have publications of their own. If some specialty attracts your attention, check the library or some area stamp club or dealer to see if there is a group which shares your interest. If nothing else, you may be able to learn of collectors with similar interests in other parts of the country and can arrange some swaps with them by mail.

7
First-Day Covers

The collecting of first-day covers is a growing part of the hobby of stamp collecting. As explained in the Introduction, first-day cover collecting offers an interesting and inexpensive way to provide a new twist to your collecting.

Whenever a new U.S. stamp is released, it is generally placed on sale first in a city having some connection with the person or event being honored. The next day it is made available at some thirty thousand Postal Service offices around the nation. The post office in the city where the stamp is issued uses a special cancellation which reads "First Day of Issue." This is run across the face of the stamp and the adjacent portions of the envelope. An envelope so marked is known as a first-day cover.

Stamps produced before 1937 were not given special cancellations on the first day. However, by checking the date of cancellation against the date of issue of the stamps, it is possible to assemble a collection of earlier first-day covers.

The use of the first-day marking began in 1937 when the

three-cent stamp honoring the sesquicentennial of the Northwest Ordinance was issued. The commemorative marked 150 years since the signing of the Ordinance of 1787 which created the Northwest Territory. The special cancellation was applied on that date to 130,531 covers at Marietta, Ohio, and to 125,134 covers at New York, New York.

While we talk about one "first-day city," there have been many exceptions. The Washington Press, in its *United States Specialized Catalog of First-Day Covers*, lists issue cities and the number of covers canceled in each.

The Sullivan Expedition stamp of June 17, 1929, while not carrying a first day of issue cancel, officially went on sale in fifteen different New York communities on the same day. The Massachusetts Bay Colony commemorative of the next year had its initial sale in just two cities, Boston and Salem.

The memorial stamp for the late President John F. Kennedy was issued in Boston on May 29, 1964, and 2,003,096 first-day covers were canceled. However, the stamp was released throughout the nation on the same day and was canceled in many cities, but not with the first-day slogan. Kennedy specialists try to get as many different JFK first-day covers as possible. The only way to identify those from cities other than Boston is by the date. The stamp was also released the same day at military installations around the world; therefore there are Kennedy first-day covers with APO (Army Post Office) and FPO (Fleet Post Office) cancellations, as well as cancellations with city names. Some of the military post offices designed special cachets so that makes it easier to identify their first-day JFK covers, even though some of them came through without any special markings.

The covers canceled outside Boston vary in value, depending on the size of the city involved and the number of covers processed. It is conceivable that only a dozen or so covers might have been canceled in some small towns. Their scarcity would of course make them much more desirable, and consequently much more valuable.

Prices for first-day covers generally have risen steadily in recent years, particularly for those with attractive cachets. The observance of the bicentennial in 1976 is creating new demands for anything connected with the American Revolution era. This has been reflected in the prices for first-day covers of stamps dealing with historic events tied to the bicentennial.

Many groups design cachets as a fund-raising device. This is particularly true of philatelic organizations, but it

Cancellations

First-Day Cancellations turn up in unusual places. This one is on a poster issued by the U.S. Postal Service. It was a special cancellation used only at the National Press Club.

could work just as well for a Scout troop. Say the troop was having a twenty-fifth anniversary on November 12. Some time during the preceding summer, the group could design a cachet which shows something connected with the troop. This could be reproduced on a rubber stamp or hand-drawn on many envelopes. The envelopes then would be offered for sale. They would be stamped with an appropriate stamp— possibly a scouting issue—and mailed so as to be canceled on the anniversary date.

Watch the stamp columns for announcements about where and how to order such cachets, as they make an interesting addition to your collection. In first-day cover collecting, as in all other types of collecting, it is important to keep up with changes in collecting interests and in the procedures for acquiring material.

The Postal Service is constantly looking for ways in which to improve its efficiency and its service to customers and collectors. For some time consideration has been given to changing the way the service handles first-day covers. Here's the way it is done as of the time of this writing.

Once a first-day city is selected, the Postal Service sends a processing team to that city to handle first-day cover orders. The team arrives some time before the stamp is to be issued and begins to process orders. The date stamps are set ahead since it obviously would be impossible to get all of the cover requests canceled on the day of issue.

The orders are received, the payment removed, and the desired stamps attached to the envelopes submitted by collectors. These are then given the first-day cancellation and set aside for dispatch on the issue date. On stamps for which there is a heavy demand, it may be some weeks before all of the orders can be processed. Orders are accepted with postmarks up until midnight of the day of issue. They are then filled as fast as possible, based on the order in which they were received. Sometimes there is a shortage of help or an extra heavy demand. This could delay receipt of the covers by collectors until some weeks after the issue date. When the processing is completed, the Postal Service team returns to the home office.

This is a costly procedure and it has raised some problems through the years. Sometimes the stamp is issued in a small town and there are inadequate facilities for the processing team to set up an effective operation. It costs a great deal of money to send out the teams since they may have to go clear across the country. It may be necessary to move heavy canceling machines into an area which does not have such facilities.

As an alternative to such moves, the Postal Service has been considering a program which would have all of the processing of first-day covers done in Washington. This would not rule out having other cities designated as first-day cities; it simply would mean that the cover orders would be sent to Washington and that the cancellations would be applied in Washington, using the name of the city which ordinarily would have been the first-day city. It still would be possible to have special ceremonies in the designated city and to have a limited first-day cancellation operation there. The postal authorities will eventually decide whether to make this change, after they consider all sides of the problem.

Having processing in two places gives rise to varieties of first-day cancellations. You might see two different cancellations on first-day covers for the same stamp. That may be due to processing in two locations or to other special circumstances.

If the city name appears in a circle about the size of a quarter, chances are good you have the standard machine cancel which is applied by running the cover between rollers. If the cancellation is about the size of a half dollar, you probably have a hand cancel. This, as the name suggests, is a cancel made with a rubber stamp that the clerk hits on a stamp pad and then applies to the cover. Hand cancels generally are used on programs and other odd-sized objects on which cancellations are requested.

Ordinarily you can get a first-day cancellation on anything on which you apply a stamp. One customer stuck a stamp on his forehead and the obliging clerk stamped him "First Day of Issue."

Remember that a first-day cancellation has to be requested. It will not be applied to a letter mailed on the issue date, even if it carries the appropriate stamp, unless it has been sent through the first-day ordering channels.

As of the time of writing this book, this is the procedure to use when ordering first-day covers: Watch the stamp columns for news of an upcoming stamp or item of postal stationery. About two weeks before the issue date address an envelope to yourself. You can use an ordinary envelope or you can buy one of the "cacheted" variety from a stamp dealer.

After you have addressed the envelope to yourself, mark lightly in pencil in the upper right-hand corner the number of stamps you wish to have affixed. While the usual number is one, there are collectors who want a block of four. You can even ask for a plate block, but you are not likely to get one unless you happen to hit a sympathetic postal clerk when your cover is being processed.

Place your completed envelope, plus money order or certified check to cover cost of the stamps desired, into another envelope which you have addressed to the postmaster in the first-day city. On the lower left-hand side of the outer envelope indicate the stamps you are requesting by writing: First Day Covers, _____ Stamp.

Be sure the amount you are enclosing is adequate to cover

the first-class mailing rate. Thus, if the first-class rate is ten cents and the new stamp being issued is a five-center, it is necessary to order at least two for each cover to meet the cost of carrying the cover back to you by first class.

One exception to this rule is the ordering of new postal cards or aerogrammes. For such items you send addressed labels plus an amount designated by the Postal Service, usually a few cents over the face value of the item ordered. The first-day postmaster in the issue city then will have your address label attached to the card or aerogramme (which already has the stamp printed on it) and mailed to you after the first-day cancellation is applied.

The Postal Service will not accept stamps or personal checks in payment for the stamps you are ordering. While they tell you not to send money, it generally is safe simply to make payment in coins, particularly if you are ordering only one or two covers. Be sure the outer envelope, to the postmaster, has your return address on it. While no limit is set on the number of covers you may order, the Postal Service says it will not accept orders for an "unreasonable" amount. This restriction generally is aimed at commercial firms rather than individual collectors.

Do not include orders for uncanceled stamps with your orders for first-day covers, as such requests will not be honored.

Famous Names

Autographs add to the value and interest of souvenir covers. This one, from the Christmas 1970 series, is signed by Tricia Nixon. The folder from the Beautification Stamp of 1966 bears the signature of Lady Bird Johnson.

CHRISTMAS 1970

BEAUTIFICATION OF AMERICA
COMMEMORATIVE STAMP PROGRAM

The White House
WASHINGTON, D.C.
October 5, 1966

When addressing your inner envelope, put your address in the lower right hand corner as far down as possible. Use a pencil to address the envelope, or buy some peel-off labels at a stamp store. Some collectors want unaddressed covers, so you may want to erase an address or peel one off before making a trade. Still another reason for writing the address low on the envelope is to allow adequate space for the stamp and cancellation. Many U.S. stamps are large and take up much of the envelope space, especially if you are ordering a block of four. Don't try to beat the system by sending in unaddressed covers as they will not be processed.

It is a good idea to put a filler of some kind in the envelope. This can be a piece of cardboard cut to the right size. This insures that you will be given a clear cancellation when the cover goes through the cancellation machine and that your cover will not be bent in the process. Do not seal the inner envelope, simply tuck in the flap. When your cover comes back you can remove the cardboard filler and use it again for your next cover order.

Up until 1974 the Postal Service would allow only one cancellation on an envelope. The new rules allow for multiple cancellations on an envelope, when the cancellations are applied at philatelic events. This means that if you have a first-day cover from some years back, you can take it with you to a first-day ceremony, add one of the new stamps and have the cover get another first-day cancel. This could be used on a statehood anniversary cover with a new cancellation applied for the new anniversary. The rules also permit the postal clerk to apply the cancellation at any point on the envelope instead of just in the upper right-hand corner as in the past.

The Postal Service has no way of tracing covers which are lost in the mail. If you have not received your covers by three weeks after the stamp has been issued, write to the postmaster in the first-day city. Tell him the way in which the cover was addressed and the number of stamps it was to have and describe the cachet or special markings.

Lost covers ordinarily will be replaced, as will those damaged by the Postal Service. Strange things happen to covers. Sometimes they are damaged in the canceling machine. Other times you will find your local post office has applied another cancellation on top of the special first-day cancel, rendering the cover worthless. In such cases, return the damaged cover to the postmaster in the first-day city and it will be replaced. Postal Service rules say they will be replaced with plain white envelopes, but cachet envelopes often are used. To be on the safe side, enclose a cacheted envelope along with your damage complaint and the cover will be processed like a new order.

As of this writing, the United States does not have a service charge for processing first-day covers. The United Nations, Canada, and several other areas do have such a charge. The imposition of such a fee could be one of the possible changes made by the U.S. when and if it revises the first-day cover program.

Sending for your own first-day covers is not always the cheapest way to get them. By the time you figure the cost of the envelopes and the postage you have to pay to send in your order, it might be cheaper and it certainly would be easier and safer simply to buy the covers from a dealer. It is possible to enter a subscription with a dealer which will automatically get you a first-day cover every time a new stamp is issued. This guarantees you won't miss any issues and it frees you of the need to prepare and submit the order. The Postal Service does not sell any first-day covers after the initial distribution. Such covers are available only through stamp dealers.

It is important to remember here that we are talking only about United States first-day covers. The procedure for ordering foreign first-day covers is similar but a bit more complicated. As mentioned earlier, some countries have a service charge. There also is the danger of loss. Mail in many foreign countries does not enjoy the security it has in the United States. Any envelope, especially if it looks as though it contains money, could easily be the target of a thief. This means it is wise to register envelopes containing money sent overseas for first-day covers. This is a costly process. Once again, when you are buying only a few covers, it is safer and cheaper to go through a dealer.

If you have certain foreign countries in which you are interested, write a letter to the postmaster general of the country and ask for its procedures on ordering first-day covers. It may work best to get a few friends together with you on your cover orders for either U.S. or foreign stamps. By combining your order you can split the cost of postage, and registry if it is required.

Experiment with your first-day collecting. Create your own cachets and get first-day cancels on unusual items like pictures, posters and folders.

8
Stamp Dealers

Your nearby stamp dealer can be a friend and counselor to you as you advance in stamp collecting. He is not only a source of stamps and supplies, but also of information from which you can draw as you probe the mysteries of philately. Stop and consider some of the reasons why a stamp dealer can be a helpful friend to you.

He deals with many collectors and they have a wide variety of interests. He keeps up with those interests in order to serve his customers, and this makes him aware of what is going on in the stamp world and among stamp collectors in your community.

He can tell you about area stamp clubs, where and when they meet, which are the best for new collectors, and how to go about joining. He can put you in touch with other collectors who have interests similar to yours. Because he is familiar with stamp publications, he can recommend which would be best for you and he can show you where to send for sample copies so you can see several types before you make a choice.

It is a good idea to introduce yourself to the stamp dealer. Tell him who you are, what you plan to collect, the size of your collection and of your stamp budget, your address and phone number. This makes it possible for him to know of your special interests and to give you a call when he gets in some stamps he thinks you might want to add to your collection.

When you have trouble identifying a stamp, the stamp dealer is a logical person to run to for help. Since he makes a business of selling stamps, he has to be able to make absolute identification of each stamp and not just guess at where it might be from or where it goes in an album.

Your dealer will sell you a perforation gauge or a watermark detector. He also will show you how to use them.

His display of albums will make you aware of what is available. If you tell him your collecting interests, he will help you pick the album best suited to your needs.

The stamp dealer keeps track of when album supplements are published. Ask him when the updating pages will be available for your particular album. Smaller dealers do not stock the annual supplements for all albums, but most dealers will be glad to order the supplements for you.

His counters offer a wide array of accessories of interest to the collector. This is a good time to begin thinking about the extra collecting tools you are ready to acquire. A good magnifying glass is something you might want to consider at this time. It is a useful tool when you are examining stamps for defects or are separating varieties of stamps which have only minor differences.

Bargain hunting is an essential part of the fun of stamp collecting. The counter at your stamp store is a good place to begin. Usually you will find several boxes of mixtures offered at a few cents per stamp. These generally are odds and ends left over after the dealer has sorted through a collection. They also could be surplus of one kind or another, or just a batch of stamps in which the dealer has lost interest. The stamps are sold individually, so you have an opportunity to look through and buy only the ones you need.

If you have a record of the stamps you require for your collection, you may find them in such mixtures. Those you find will come to you at a fraction of the cost you would have to meet if you picked them from a stock book.

Your stamp dealer can be helpful when you want to get rid of your duplicate stamps. Don't expect a big profit if you take him a pile of common stamps. But, if you talk to him ahead of time, you may be able to arrange to swap some of your duplicates for credit toward the stamps you need. This is particularly true if you get many foreign stamps and are interested in collecting only U.S. issues.

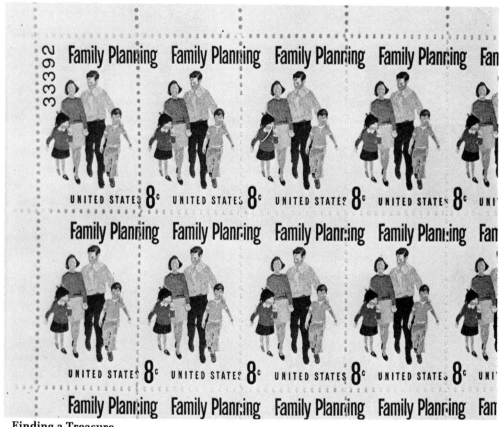

Finding a Treasure

Look closely at the stamps you buy. This printing error has left the first row of stamps without any denomination and has produced a philatelic oddity worth hundreds of dollars.

Pick up a price list while you are at the shop. It lets you know the prices charged by the dealer and usually outlines procedures for ordering by mail. Sometimes the lists are free; other times a charge is made and then deducted from the first order. The price list can serve a dual function. It lets you know what the stamps you want are going to cost, and you also can use it as a check list to keep track of the stamps you have and the stamps you need.

The amount of attention a stamp dealer will be able to give you will depend to a great extent on the time of your visit. If you go into his store on Saturday when he has many customers, he probably will do little more than hand you a price list. If you go in on a weekday or during hours when he is not busy, he will be more likely to spend some time with you. You may even get to watch him sort some stamps, and thus get some tips on how to improve your own stamp processing.

Most stamp dealers developed a business from their hobby. They still retain their interest in talking about and working with stamps even when they are not selling them. Such a dealer can add much to the enjoyment of your hobby.

Young collectors who get ignored by stamp dealers often invite such treatment. If you are with a group that is noisy or disturbing other customers in the shop, you will not be welcome. If you handle the merchandise carelessly or pick up items and move them from place to place in the shop you will arouse suspicion. Stamp dealers are preyed upon by shoplifters. They may therefore be unwilling to let you sort through their stock books on your own, at least, not until they get to know you. The quicker you can convince them you are a sincere collector, the quicker you will earn their trust and cooperation.

Some stamp dealers are glad to offer discounts to their regular customers. If the dealer knows you and sees you in his shop regularly, he may extend such benefits to you.

Don't ask for credit. You won't get it since the dealer would have no way of collecting should you decide not to pay. He has ways to make adults pay, but he has no such legal approach to juveniles. If you want to tie your stamp spending to your allowance, then ask your parents to talk to the stamp dealer and tell him the limits up to which they will be responsible for your spending.

If you try to sell stamps to a dealer, you can expect to be challenged if you offer him any rare or valuable stamps. Once again, the problem is a legal one. The dealer has no way of knowing where you got the stamps or whether you have the right to sell them. Suppose they were part of a stamp album given to you by your grandfather and some of them duplicated stamps already in your album. You might decide you want to sell some of them to get money to buy the other stamps you need. The thing to do is to get a letter from a parent or responsible adult which states that the stamps are yours and that you have permission to sell them. This assures the dealer the stamps have not been stolen and he is free to make a deal with you.

The price you pay for stamps from a dealer is determined largely by the amount of work the dealer has to do for you. Stamps are cheapest when bought in unsorted bulk lots called mixtures. This gives you stamps in basically the same condition as the batch you started with when you began accumulating stamps from "free" sources. In selling these stamps to you, the dealer has had to do nothing but buy them in quantity and then weigh them out in lots for resale. Obviously some dealers will go through and remove the better stamps. However, there generally is enough value left to make this an inexpensive and acceptable way to buy stamps.

Generally these are used stamps, but the mixtures can include unused stamps as well. Once your collection begins to grow, such bulk buying becomes less of a bargain for you since you will be getting many duplicates. However, such purchases occasionally still are fun as they give you a few hours' pleasure and a good assortment of duplicates for trading purposes.

Each step the dealer has to take after that will increase the price you pay for the stamps you buy. If he soaks the stamps off the paper, your cost goes up. We live in a time when labor costs are increasing. It no longer is possible for stamp dealers to find people who will soak stamps off paper for very little money. There was a time when the biggest stamp dealers shipped millions of stamps overseas to have them soaked off the paper, since it was cheaper to pay the shipping and labor costs than it would have been to have the work done in the United States. The stamps often were soaked in large tubs and then spread on the grass to dry. American-trained supervisors showed the native workers how to press and process the stamps before they were returned to the United States. Some of the stamps in the packets you buy today may have been soaked in that fashion.

Now that living standards and wages have climbed in foreign countries, overseas labor no longer is the bargain it once was. As a result, more of the soaking is being done in the United States. The dealers have to pay at least a minimum wage. This means their costs go up and the increase is passed on to you in the form of higher stamp prices.

As we discuss each of these steps, remember that none of them adds anything to the value of the stamp, only to the cost. When you get around to selling or trading a stamp from your collection, you won't, of course, add anything to cover the cost of the work done for you by the stamp dealer. This makes the "do-it-yourself" part of the hobby important from an economy standpoint if for no other reason.

We talked about the sorting process in an earlier chapter.

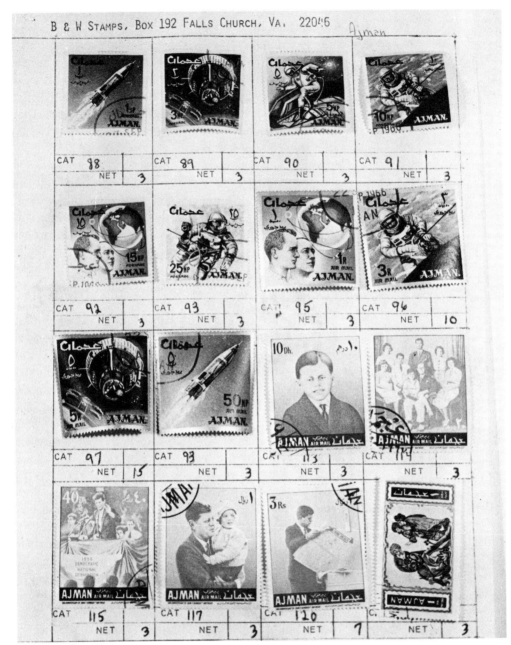

Pick and Pay

Approval buyers are offered a selection of individually priced stamps. They select and pay for the ones they want and return the others to the dealer.

Your cost for stamps will go up again if the dealer has to do the sorting for you. If he mounts the stamps in counter display books or makes them up in packets, you can expect to absorb the added costs of such processing.

When the dealer sends out stamps on approval, the customer has to pay the mailing costs both ways, plus a portion of the money the dealer loses when other customers fail to return his approval selections. While these costs may not appear to be added to the price when you purchase the stamps, you may be sure they are reflected in the total price you are paying.

As you advance in collecting, it will be impractical for you to buy many stamps in bulk or ready-made packets, as you will be getting too many duplicates. At that point you will begin to work with "want lists" of the stamps you need and will be able to look for them in auctions, dealer stock books, and in swaps with other collectors.

There are exceptions to this. Two such exceptions are the purchase of mission mixtures or kiloware. Mission mixtures are supposed to be stamps removed from envelopes received by charitable organizations. These stamps usually are sold by the pound. Occasionally you will find a group which provides a truly unsorted mixture in which you can find some good stamps. Too often the stamps will have been thoroughly checked over to remove high values, commemoratives and oddities, for sale separately at a higher price.

A tip-off can be the price of the mixture. If it seems too cheap, it probably is not much of a bargain. The best approach is to try one mixture and see if you like what you get. You can always reorder if you are satisfied. Some firms advertise money-back guarantees if you are not satisfied. If they make such a promise and then refuse to refund your money, complain to the publication in which the ad appeared and a refund usually will be arranged.

In fairness to yourself and to the stamp dealer, read the ads carefully before you mail in an order. Be sure you understand what the ad promises, not what you would like to think it promises. An advertisement for a "world-wide mixture" could and probably would include many common U.S. stamps. If you want only foreign stamps, be sure that the ad says that is what you will get.

Careful stamp shopping also includes an awareness of the importance of condition. Be realistic in your purchases. You have to expect to pay more for a stamp that is in perfect condition than you would pay for one with a perforation missing or a thin spot on the back or a heavy cancellation. If you are buying mint stamps, you will pay more for those with the gum undisturbed than for those which have been hinged. Ask your dealer to show you examples of the various conditions which change the value of stamps.

The purchase of kiloware is somewhat different than the

buying of a mission mixture. It is a system used by some foreign governments to add to their postal revenues. Stamps are gathered from government sources, such as tax offices, official mail and special charity stamp sales. These are bundled, weighed and offered to the public in "kilo" lots.

A kilo is equal to 2.2 pounds. The price for a kilo varies from country to country and depends in part on the kind of material it contains. Some kiloware consists primarily of commemorative stamps and sells at a much higher price than a kilo containing many stamps of lower values. Kiloware from a country which does not issue many stamps will sell for a higher price than kiloware from a country which turns out a large volume of stamps.

The number of stamps in a kilo will vary according to the size of the stamps, the amount of paper to which they are attached, and the closeness of the trim around the edge. Ordinarily there will be about three thousand stamps in a kilo.

In most cases the price of the kilo is set by the government involved, but sometimes the price is set by an annual auction in which offers are solicited and then the stamps are sold, beginning with the highest bid and continuing down the line until the supply is exhausted.

Kiloware often can be purchased directly from the governments involved. It also can be acquired through dealers who buy up large lots and then resell them. New lots are made up each year and the ones left over from previous years are offered by some stamp dealers. Kilos are sealed by the governments that make them up, so the customer is protected against further screening out of valuable stamps by middlemen.

Information on the availability of kiloware can be found in stamp columns or in stamp publications. Look over the advertisements and find the best price. If neither source gives you the information you want, check with your stamp dealer.

Buying stamps in this fashion is not recommended for an individual unless you plan to do a great deal of trading or have extra time to spend soaking and sorting. The reason for this is the large number of duplicates you get in such a lot. It is, however, a good idea for a club or group of collectors to buy such a mixture and process it together and then share the stamps. Your stamp dealer also may be willing to buy some of the duplicates after you have soaked and sorted them.

Whether you order by mail or buy over the counter from a stamp dealer, you have a responsibility for fair and honest dealings. Treat the merchandise with care. Buy what you want, pay for it and return the unwanted material within a reasonable time. Abuse of these rules means that the next buyer will have to pay more for his or her stamps, and that next buyer could be you.

9
Auctions

Buying and selling are important parts of any hobby which involves collecting. This is particularly true of stamp collecting.

You have progressed through the accumulation stage; you have learned about buying from dealers and how to read and understand stamp advertising. We have talked about catalogs and how to use them as the basis for exchanges of stamps with other collectors. Let's look now at the interesting and exciting world of auctions as a means of adding to your own collection or disposing of your duplicates.

Auction selling dates back many years. In early times it was a quick way of settling a debt. The possessions of a person who owed money were put on a block and sold to the highest bidder. The money realized from the sale was used to pay off the person to whom the money was owed. The auctioneer got his cut. What was left, if anything, was given to the owner of the auctioned property.

Over the years auctions have continued to attract crowds

of buyers, sellers, and the just plain curious. It was inevitable that auction activity would become part of the hobby field as well.

If you are in an organized stamp club, the chances are good that you have auctions as part of the regular meeting program. If your club does not have such sales, then steps should be taken to get them started. It is not a complicated process. Members are invited to bring in material they wish to sell. Generally this consists of packets of stamps, or of individual stamps or covers if they are of higher value. The seller presents his packet together with a description of it to the auctioneer before the meeting. The packets, or "lots" as they are called in auctions, are put on display. Other members are able to look over the items before being asked to bid on them. The seller indicates the lowest amount he is willing to accept for his lot. Many times the items are put up for sale with no minimum bid.

The size of the club will play a part in determining how the auction will proceed from this point. If you have about fifteen people attending your meeting, this is enough to have a good lively auction. Choose one member of the club to be the auctioneer. This should be a person who is not afraid to stand up in front of the group. A good auctioneer is a showman and can add excitement to the sale as he calls out the bids until a sale is made.

The auction begins with the auctioneer saying something like: "Our first lot consists of two hundred different United States commemorative stamps. These stamps all are used and have a total catalog value of six dollars. Most of them were issued in the last ten years. The owner asks a minimum bid of twenty-five cents. Do I hear a quarter?"

Club rules determine the bidding from that point. Ordinarily bids are increased in steps of five cents each until one dollar is reached, then in ten-cent steps until two dollars is reached and in steps of twenty-five cents each after that.

The auctioneer continues the sale, announcing each new bid until there are no more offers. He then says the traditional: "Going . . . going . . . gone!" after which the item is handed to the buyer.

Before your auction gets under way, it is necessary to pick one club member to keep track of the buyers and another to keep a record of the sellers. Settlement for the lots sold is made after the meeting.

Clubs generally charge a small percentage of the sale

price as an auction fee. This money is put into the club treasury and can be used to buy door prizes or refreshments for future meetings.

Let's assume that the typical lot we talked about earlier sold for $2.00. The person recording the buyers would make a note of this so as to collect $2.00 from the purchaser at the end of the meeting. The person keeping tab on the sellers would record a sale of $2.00, deduct a sales fee of 10 cents (five percent of the selling price) and turn $1.90 over to the seller at the end of the meeting.

If no one is willing to make a minimum bid, the items are returned to the seller, who can either reduce the minimum asking price or simply take back the stamps and hold them for the next auction.

While bidding normally is done by calling out the price you are willing to pay, this is not always the case. A skilled auctioneer looks around the room constantly. He spots a raised finger, a tilted head, or even a wink of the eye telling him that the person is willing to bid more than the last offer.

Curb your enthusiasm before you get into a serious auction. It is too easy to get caught up in the excitement of bidding and end up paying considerably more than you intended for an item. You usually have a chance to examine the sale lots ahead of time and get an idea of what they are worth. Set in your mind the amount you are willing to pay and don't let your bidding get beyond that amount. Look over all the items in the auction. You may find two or more similar lots. Don't overbid on the first lot when you may be able to buy the same material for less later on.

Less formal and more novel auction approaches are possible, particularly if you are a member of a small club. Here's one variation. Club members sit around a table. The lots to be sold are put in cigar boxes and passed around the table, one lot per box. The person seated at the head of the table acts as the auctioneer.

When a box reaches your place at the table, you examine the contents and decide if you want to bid. You get only one chance. You write your bid on a paper, together with your name or initials, fold it up and drop it in the box. The next person getting the box does the same thing without getting to look at your bid. When the box has gone completely around the table the bids are opened and the stamps are sold to the highest bidder.

A variation on this idea is to impose a penalty on the person submitting the lowest bid. The penalty could be small, just a few cents, this being awarded to the person submitting the second highest bid. This discourages people from bidding too low. It means the seller gets a better price and the bidder has the added challenge of guessing not only what price the stamps will sell for, but what the others will bid.

There is a kind of reverse bidding auction which also can be fun. This involves starting with a high figure and working downward. Any club member can say "stop" at any point and buy the item at that price. The challenge comes in trying to decide how far down you can let the price go before someone else decides to buy the stamp you want. If two or more people say "stop" at the same time, the bidding goes back up until only one person is willing to pay the price.

Up to now we have been talking about auctions where you are physically present in the room where a sale is being held. In philately there are several ways to buy at auction without being present.

Many stamp dealers employ a system of stock books where stamps are offered for sale in another kind of auction. A person wanting to sell stamps mounts them on a page provided by the dealer, identifies the stamp by catalog number and value and lists the minimum acceptable bid. Both the seller and potential buyers use code numbers provided by the dealer for identification. In this way, neither the buyer nor the seller is able to identify each other just by looking at the page.

These auction stock books are kept available on the counter at the stamp store, usually for about three weeks. Customers come in and look at the pages. If they see something they want, they look at the bottom of the page and see what the last bidder offered for the stamps. If they want to go higher, they put their identification number and the amount they are willing to pay on the page. On a particularly popular stamp or cover there could be dozens of bids over the three-week period. At the end of that time the stamp dealer holds an auction in his shop. He begins the bidding for each item with the highest price written on the page. If anyone in the shop wants to bid more he gets the stamps. If there are no "shop" bids, then the person who made the highest bid on the page is notified to come in and pick up the stamps. New books are added each week, so there always are new stamps and covers from which to choose.

The best way to use this kind of auction is to have a list of the catalog numbers of the stamps in which you are interested and the price you would have to pay for them if you bought them directly from a dealer's stock instead of at auction. On the day of the sale, look through the books for the items you decided you wanted and check the highest bid. If it is below what you would normally have to pay for the stamp, then show up at the auction and you just might pick up a bargain. A little later in this chapter we will talk about putting your duplicates up for sale in the auction.

A kind of stamp auction which is growing in popularity is the mail auction. There are a number of firms, both large and small, which offer philatelic material through sales of this type. Some of the larger ones issue sales catalogs months in advance of the sale. These catalogs, which are nothing more than a list and perhaps pictures of the items to be sold, give you a chance to see what is offered and to decide if you want it for your collection. It is important to read these catalogs carefully as they tell you much about the condition of the items on which you will be bidding. "Slight thin" or "small tear" tells you that you are bidding on a damaged stamp and your bid should be adjusted accordingly.

When bidding in a mail sale, the normal procedure is to indicate the maximum amount you are willing to pay for the stamp offered. When the actual sale is held, the auctioneer will have an assistant who will have a record of all of the bids that have come in by mail. This will be used to compete with the bidders who come to the sale in person. Suppose you wanted a particular stamp and have indicated you are willing to pay up to ten dollars for it. If the next highest bid is $8.00, then the auctioneer's assistant would enter your bid of $8.25, which is the next normal bid. If there were no other bids, the stamp would be sold to you for $8.25. Your bid will be no higher than it has to be to get the item and it will not go over the limits you have set. You do not send money to bid in a mail auction. When the sale is over you are notified if you submitted the highest bid and are told how much to send. The stamps are sent to you when the money is received. In most sales of this type you have a few days to look over the stamps to be sure you are getting the stamps as advertised. If, for instance, you were led to believe you were bidding on the watermarked variety of a given stamp and you found the stamps sent to you were unwatermarked, you would be entitled to a refund. The same thing would be true if you received damaged stamps and no mention of the damage had been made in the sales catalog.

We have been talking about how you buy stamps from auctions. Let's take a look at the process to follow when you have stamps to sell.

Auctions involve competitive bidding. They are transactions in which the buyers are looking for a bargain and do not want to pay the full price for the stamps they are buying. It is important to keep this in mind when you set minimum prices on the lots you put in an auction. If your minimum bid requirement is too high, you will not sell the item since there will be no bidders. If your minimum bid is too low, you may never get it up to a fair price for the material you have for sale. Be realistic in your pricing. If a dealer will sell a certain stamp for a quarter, don't put that stamp in an auction and make the minimum bid a quarter. Chances are good you won't get it if you do.

Talk to more experienced collectors and ask them what they think would be a fair asking price. Some countries are much more popular with collectors than other countries. The stamps of the popular areas can be expected to bring more at auction for the same reasons they cost more at the stamp counter.

The key lies in knowing two things: the value of the material you have for sale and the kind of group to which you are going to offer it for sale. If your group is made up of youngsters with limited budgets, chances are good you aren't going to sell much at a high price. If you are a member of an adult group and are a new collector, there is little likelihood your packet of duplicate recent issues will attract much attention or bids.

For club auctions, be a watcher instead of a seller or a buyer at the first few meetings you attend. Take a look at the kind of material being offered and at the kind that is being bought. If there seems to be an interest in topical collecting, then you probably can come up with a good lot of topicals from your duplicates. If there are plate block collectors in the group, then save the plate blocks from your next trip to the post office and offer them in the auction. Try to put in the auction something a little different from what is being offered by everyone else. If all you see in the auction display are packets of stamps, then try to offer a few covers from your collection. Any letters you get from overseas can make an interesting lot, even business letters with unusual stamps on them. These are called commercial covers and usually attract interest at an auction.

In Chapter Seven we talked about making your own cachets for first-day covers. Items of this type are popular in auctions and you have the advantage of knowing that no one else will be offering exactly the same thing you are. Keep this in mind when you send for first-day covers and make up a few extras. They are good for trading as well as for auctions.

If all you have to offer are routine stamps, you still can improve your chances for a sale by clever packaging. Keep an eye out for unusual containers coming into the house. A wooden cigar box containing a few hundred stamps will sell for more if you describe it as a "pirate's treasure chest" and paint it black or put some skull-and-crossbone stickers on it. A window-front envelope with some flashy stamps showing through has a better chance to sell than just a box of loose stamps. A cover about which you can provide a bit of the history becomes much more salable. If the auctioneer is able to say, "This is a cover which was carried on the first flight from Philadelphia to Harrisburg, Pennsylvania," he is much more likely to get bids than if he merely says, "This is a first-flight cover."

If you are going to be a regular member of a club and contribute to club auctions, then take steps early to develop and preserve your reputation as a good collector. If you put envelopes of stamps in the auction, be sure the buyer doesn't find a bunch of damaged stamps at the back of the envelope. You might get away with a trick like this once or twice, but members will soon learn to avoid your items in future sales.

If you plan to participate in the mail sales, use one of them as a means of learning about the procedures. Write for the rules and a catalog of the items to be offered. At the same time request a report on the prices realized. There may be a small charge for this service, but it is a good investment. What you get after the sale is a list showing you how much was paid for each item. You can use this as a handy guide for deciding the minimum price you want to ask for items you might put in a future sale. In setting your price, or in buying for that matter, it is important to remember that auction houses charge a fee for conducting the sales and the seller gets only part of the selling price, a commission going to the auction house. This means the asking price must take this added expense into account.

Mail auctions are not the cheapest way to buy stamps, but they are useful. They often turn up scarce items which normally are not found on a dealer's shelves. Sometimes an auction house gets hold of an estate and is able to offer entire collections. These sometimes are broken up. Other times they are sold as a unit.

If you live in a metropolitan area, check with your post office to see if there will be a "dead letter auction" in the near future in your area. Each year thousands of letters and packets are found to be undeliverable. This may be due to damage in shipping, incorrect addresses, lost labels or any number of other reasons. When this happens, the packages are sent to a central collecting point. Several times a year the articles are auctioned at public sale. Generally they are placed on display for a day or two before the sale and then are sold at auction. There is usually some philatelic material among the items offered. Often this consists of approvals which were lost in the mail; shipments from stamp companies which went out of business; packets of stamps which broke open in the mail; or shipments of stamps made to persons who had not ordered them and would not pay the postage to send them back.

Sales of this type are fun but they are not always bargains. The stamps in a damaged parcel may have gotten wet in the proces and be all stuck together. There may only be a few stamps you want but you have to buy the entire lot to get the ones you need. Perhaps most important, the sales are frequented by two groups of people who make it difficult for you to find a real "treasure." First of these are the professional auction buyers. While they probably are not at the sale primarily for the stamps, they will not let a real bargain get past them. The other group is made up of the auction-happy crowds who just like the fun of bidding and usually are willing to pay more than an item is worth.

How does it all add up? Auctions are a fun way to get the stamps you need and occasionally you can get them at a price well below the market value. The key is in keeping yourself informed. You need to be aware of the stamps you have and the stamps you need. You will want to know what it would cost you to buy the stamps from a dealer and you will want to know how hard it will be to find the stamps when you want them if you don't buy them now.

From a club standpoint, auctions add excitement and interest as well as providing a reason for going to the meetings. A good auctioneer can liven up a club meeting even if the material offered for sale is not exceptional.

10
Stamp Clubs

As your involvement in stamp collecting grows, you will want to share that involvement with others of similar interests. The best way to do so is by joining or forming a stamp club. Let's talk first about the advantages of joining an existing club. This gives you a meeting place where you can share ideas, display your collection, swap or buy stamps and talk about problems you encounter in collecting. It introduces you to stamp shows, stamp auctions, and special club programs.

Your local newspaper stamp column is a good place to look for information about stamp clubs in your area. Your library or your stamp dealer also should be able to provide this information. They probably can tell you where the various groups meet and give you some idea of the activities of the members. If you live in a metropolitan area, you will have a wider variety of clubs from which to choose. They range from large informal groups to small specialized societies. Look them over carefully.

Not all clubs welcome new collectors, particularly when

the collectors are both new and young. Many of the members of the more organized groups take their collecting very seriously. You have to walk softly when you enter their area. While some club members might resent your intrusion and your questions, other members will welcome you. It is only by shopping around that you will find the club best suited to your interests and your needs.

You can get a clue about a club from looking at the announcements it puts out about its meetings. If they publicize the appearance of an expert who will talk about the technical aspects of local postmarks on the stamps of early China, chances are good you would be lost in a club of this type. If their announcement says something simple like "meeting, auc-

Club Publications

Clubs form to meet the special interests of collectors. Some of the larger clubs put out elaborate publications dealing with their specialties.

tion, swaps," this probably is more what you want for the present.

Talk to members of existing groups and ask them about their clubs. Chances are they will be glad to tell you about the one they belong to and to suggest that you come to a meeting. This, obviously, is the best way to find out about a club. When you arrive, introduce yourself to one or more of the members and ask for some information about the group. In short order you will know how often and where the club meets; what some of the members collect; and what goes on at a meeting.

Be a participant, but don't try to take over at the first meeting you attend. Unless you are in a junior club, or in the junior segment of an adult club, you risk irritating some of the older members and this could reduce your enjoyment of club activities. When you ask questions, ask about things which really concern you, don't just ask for the sake of asking. Show interest in the collections of others. This will get them talking about their collections and about your collection. Such conversation leads to swaps and shared experiences, and thus to greater enjoyment of the hobby.

Suppose, for some reason, you cannot find a club to your liking in your area. There are many circumstances under which this could happen. You might be in a small town. You might not be free on the meeting nights of the established clubs; the meeting place could be too far from your home; or the interests of the members could be too advanced for you. Then you should think about forming your own club.

Whenever two or more people get together to swap, sell or just talk about stamps, you have the basic elements for a stamp club. Get a few more collectors together, or even a few noncollector friends who might get interested. Such a group could be gathered at a school or church, a Scout troop, or just around the neighborhood. Agree with them on some simple rules such as when and where the club will meet; who will be invited to join; and what you will do at the meetings. You can pick officers if you want them, but this is not essential, at least not in the earliest stages of the club.

A good way to start is with a club project. A stamp soaking session works very well in this situation. Divide up the jobs so that each member gets a chance to do some soaking, some drying and some sorting. Divide up the results so that each member also gets some of the stamps.

Each member or potential member should be encouraged to talk about his or her collecting ideas, as this helps the members to get to know and enjoy each other. It also lets them know which member to contact when they want to trade stamps from a certain area.

Stamp swapping is a club activity which can begin at the very first meeting and be a regular part of subsequent meetings. It can be done in many ways. You can make up packets of your duplicates and offer to trade twenty-five of your stamps for twenty-five of those of some other member. The size of the packet is up to the individual collector. It is advisable to keep the number small since this lets you see more readily what you are getting so you can decide if you want to make the trade.

As you learned in the chapter on catalogs, each stamp has an assigned catalog value. That value can, within limits, be used as a basis for stamp swaps. This is true if material of a comparable kind is exchanged, for instance, medium grade U.S. for medium grade U.S., France for France, Latin America for Latin America.

Some collectors like to put their duplicate stamps in loose-leaf notebooks and price each stamp. If several collectors in a group use this method, the members have an opportunity to "shop" among the books. One member picks a dollar's worth out of your book and then you are able to pick the same amount from his or her book.

Auctions provide another club activity which makes it possible to dispose of your duplicate stamps or acquire stamps provided by other members. Since auctions are discussed in detail in Chapter Nine, we will not go into them here other than to say that a regular auction adds excitement and interest to your meetings.

One-for-one swaps add the element of treasure hunting to your stamp trading. Bring in a box of loose stamps and ask other members to do the same. Let them go through your box and select the stamps they want. Count the stamps they have taken and then you go through and pick a like number from their boxes. The more members you have in your club and the more boxes, the better the opportunity to find the stamps you need for your collection.

Spread the word about your group. Make up little posters and put them on the bulletin boards at school. Ask the scoutmaster to make an announcement about your club at his next meeting. Send a small notice to the editor of the local paper telling about the club and giving a telephone number to call for more information. Talk to the other youngsters who live on your street and invite them to come to a meeting to see what goes on. All of these things create interest and can be an effective means of attracting new members.

Your meetings should be scheduled on a regular basis. This gets members in the habit of planning to attend at the same time each week. It usually is a good idea to avoid weekends since there are too many other activities competing for your time.

The meetings do not always have to be in the same place. They can move around at the homes of the members or they can be at the library, the school, the church or the recreation center.

When a new member joins your club, be sure that he or she is made to feel welcome. The person bringing in the new member should introduce him or her to the group and tell a little bit about the kind of collecting in which he or she is interested. After that the common interests of the members will take over and the newcomer soon becomes part of the group.

The kind of activities carried on by your club will depend in part on the number of members, the age of the members, and the degree to which you want to get involved in formal procedures. Some groups will want to have officers, keep minutes and have regular business meetings. Others will want informal gatherings without a regular program.

Leaders emerge in any group and you will have a "president," whether or not anyone actually holds the title. If you have dues, you are going to need a treasurer to keep track of the money. If auctions are a regular part of your meetings, then you will need an auctioneer.

The amount of interest in the club will guide you in the direction you need to move if the club is to keep going. If the members are satisfied with informal meetings where you just swap and talk about stamps, then this is enough for the present. When the interest lags, and it will after the members all have seen all of the stamps of the other members, you will have to take some steps to keep the members coming back or recruit new members who will bring new interest and new swapping material.

When you reach this point, you might want to consider charging dues. The amount could be small, but it could pay off in more ways than just putting some money into the club treasury. Members who pay dues, even small dues, are more likely to attend regularly and be more interested than members who just show up because they haven't anything better to do.

The money collected can be used to buy mixtures and put them into swap boxes as described earlier. It also can be used to buy catalogs or other items for the club. Perhaps some of it could be used for the purchase of door prizes which are an excellent way to boost attendance at meetings. The prizes can be small—a pair of tongs, a package of hinges, a packet of stamps, a perforation gauge. Put the names of all club members into a box and draw out a winner. Make a rule that a member must be present to win. If the winner is not present, the prize can be held over until the next meeting, or another name can be drawn. Those who lose out by being absent soon will get the message and begin showing up at future meetings.

Club trips are another way to keep interest alive. Try a visit to a stamp show, a museum or even a stamp shop. If you are going to a stamp shop, go during a period when the owner is not busy. Arrange the visit ahead of time and he will be able to display some special material which might be of interest to your group.

One of your field trips could be to a meeting of one of the organized clubs in your area. Let them know ahead of time that you are coming and they may prepare a special program for you.

On your field trip to the library check out the supply of stamp publications and any special stamp programs they may have scheduled. Look over the publications and see if your group would like to subscribe to one of them. It is a good idea to use some of your club treasury for this purpose since you need a source of information on new issues and other stamp activities. The publication could be ordered in the name of one of the club members and delivered to his or her home. It then could be circulated among other members of the club, with each allowed to keep it a few days.

You might want to invite a more experienced collector to visit your club. Such a collector could talk about some collecting angles which might be new to the members. He could, for instance, show how to distinguish early U.S. issues by marks in the corners of the stamps. The opportunities for other subjects to be discussed are virtually unlimited. There could be a discussion of how to use a catalog or how to identify the stamps of a foreign country.

One thing you will discover about stamp collectors is that most of them like to talk about stamps. Many adult collectors are interested in young collectors and their collections. You can take advantage of that interest to get some valuable help for your club.

You don't always have to go outside the club to find ways in which to keep the meetings interesting. You have a number of members, each with different collecting interests and different approaches to collecting. This usually means they have different albums or different ways to mount and present their stamps. Give them all a chance to tell about their albums. Why did they choose the album they are now using? Are they happy with it? What new ways to handle their stamps have they discovered since they began collecting? How are they going about building their collections? Collectors take pride in their collections. If you give them a chance you will find them strong supporters for your club.

At some point your club will be ready to put on a stamp show. We will talk about how to approach such a project in the next chapter.

11
Stamp Shows

Somewhere in your collecting career you are going to have a chance to attend a stamp show. Be sure to take advantage of it. What you will find probably will be very different from what you expected. Stamp shows are primarily sales promotions, designed to give stamp dealers an opportunity to display their wares in front of a large group of people in a short period of time.

Most stamp shows last two or three days, usually over a weekend. In large cities they are held in armories, hotels or large halls. In smaller towns they are held in community centers, church basements, schools, libraries or any other meeting place. The largest shows usually are held in conjunction with some national philatelic observance, such as Stamp Collecting Week which comes in November of each year. They also may be held as part of community celebrations or on a regular schedule at a community center.

The stamp shows are supported primarily by the dealers who sell stamps at them. This generally means that admission

Fund Raisers

Stamp clubs can raise money for shows by preparing their own cachets. This cover was prepared by the Golden Bear Chapter of the Scouts on Stamps Society.

is free or that only a nominal fee is charged. The dealers pay a heavy charge to have booth space, particularly at the major shows. They must recoup this money before they can think about making a profit from sales at the show. As a result, prices on many items will be higher than normal.

Stamp exhibits draw the collectors to the show area and expose them to the sales by the dealers at the *bourse*. This is a word you will run across many times in your collecting. It is a French word which means money market, business or exhibition. Generally it is applied to a gathering of dealers for the purpose of conducting a sale.

The "show" part of the stamp show can be of several varieties. At the major shows some foreign countries provide displays of their stamps. The United Nations often sets up a display area showing U.N. issues and then operates a sales counter where the collectors can buy United Nations stamps and other items of philatelic interest. The United States follows a similar pattern and sometimes has a very elaborate exhibit. Such an exhibit could include a printing press or a perforating machine or some demonstration of the mechanics involved in the production of U.S. postage stamps. The United States also would be likely to have a sales counter at the major shows offering stamps, first-day covers, collector kits and similar items.

New stamps often are issued in connection with the major shows, with a first-day ceremony being held in the exhibit area. Even if new stamps or postal stationery is not issued, there are likely to be special cancellations for letters mailed at the show, and special cachets to serve as souvenirs of the show.

The number of dealers at a show will vary from a dozen or so to more than one hundred. At local shows they will be mainly dealers from the area. At the major shows there will be representatives of international firms. The producers of the best-known albums and other philatelic supplies will also be represented at the biggest shows.

Sometimes stamp and coin shows will be combined, particularly at local levels. This is done to get more dealers to participate and thereby to attract a larger crowd. When stamp and coin shows are taking place in the same hall, the dealers for coins generally are in a room separate from the dealers in stamps.

There is a way to attend a stamp show which will add to your enjoyment of it and also give you an opportunity to get the most benefit from it. If it is to be a two- or three-day show, begin by planning to attend each of the days if possible. This gives you an opportunity to map your approach carefully and also to shop in order to get the best buy for your dollar. The major shows charge admission, but generally they have a reduced rate if you buy a ticket for all three days of the show. Be sure to ask about this before you buy your ticket.

Your first visit to a stamp show will probably be confusing to you. There is a lot of activity and noise. People are milling about, there may be music or announcements on a loudspeaker.

As soon as you are inside the door, you will probably be asked to buy or will be given a program. This outlines what is going to happen at different times on each of the days. It also gives you a floor plan that shows where each of the dealers is located. Usually all the booths are numbered so it is easy to find the ones of special interest to you.

Look first at the schedule to see what events are planned. If there is to be a first-day ceremony, be sure to put it on your agenda so that you can be there when the new stamp is issued. Put one of the new stamps on your program and then have the clerk apply a first-day cancellation. This will give you a souvenir and will also give the program extra interest should you ever decide to display or sell it.

Once inside, begin by looking at the government exhibits. Try to arrive when the show opens in the morning. The crowds will be smaller and you will be able to look around at a more leisurely pace.

The major stamp organizations generally try to have their annual meetings at the big shows. They set up booths in order to try and attract new members. Often such booths will be showing a movie about stamps or some other aspects of collecting. The topical societies, for instance, may have special displays pushing the collecting of topical stamps. The postal stationery groups will try to interest you in the collecting of aerogrammes and related items. Stop and look, see the movies, take the pamphlets, but don't buy anything until closer to the end of the show. There will be many demands on your pocket during the show. That is why it is important to delay your purchases until you have had a good chance to look around.

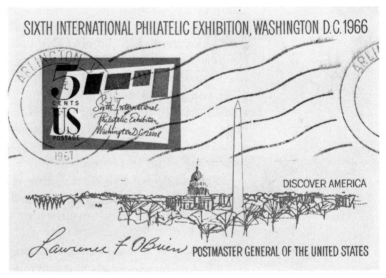

Souvenir Sheets

These special issues make an interesting addition to any stamp collection. The United States issued this sheet in 1966 as a salute to the Sixth International Philatelic Exhibition (SIPEX) which was held in Washington, D.C.

After seeing the free exhibits, make a walking tour of the dealer stands. Take note of what each has to offer. If you see a stamp or cover of special interest, make a note of the item and the dealer offering it, as well as the price. This makes it possible for you to make comparisons when you see the same type of material offered by another dealer.

Stamp shows are a good time to look for unusual or scarce items. Many stamps are scarce without being expensive because they simply are not the stamps ordinarily being displayed in a stamp store. This is especially true if you are collecting revenues, cut squares, precancels or perfins. Christmas seals and hunting permit stamps also seem to turn up at stamp shows. The dealers bring these items to a show since it is a chance for them to sell some pieces for which they normally do not have much demand.

Watch for the dealers who have few customers. This may

happen because the items they offer are not popular, or it may happen because the dealer has set his prices too high. As the show progresses, the dealers will become more and more concerned about making enough sales at least to cover the cost of their participation. On the last day it is frequently possible to get some extra bargains because of this. You may be able to make a dealer an offer considerably below his asking price and find yourself a deal. By selling to you the dealer has immediate cash, and he has also eliminated the need to repack the material and take it back to his shop.

Attending a stamp show provides other benefits besides bargains. If you see a person carefully studying some item in a display, ask him if he would mind telling you what makes the item of such special concern. Some will tell you to go away, but more will share their interest with you. The result could help you find some philatelic fact of which you had been unaware up to that point.

In going around to the various dealers you may become acquainted with one who has the kind of material you want at prices you can afford to pay. If you become friendly with him you could establish a relationship which will last through many years of collecting.

By checking the displays of the various collector organizations, you may become aware of new groups in your area. You will meet the officers of the local club and could find yourself invited to the next meeting.

Up until now we have been talking about attending a stamp show put on by someone else. Suppose you are in a small town or in an area where they do not have stamp shows. Does this mean you are to be denied the advantages of attending a show? By no means. Make a club project out of setting up your own show. You won't have the dealers or the *bourse*, but you still can have a lot of fun.

Plan your first show on a modest scale. Begin by making sure club members are interested in having a show. Find out how many are willing to participate and what they are willing to do. There are displays to be made, posters to be designed, a space to be arranged, publicity and promotion work to be done. Hopefully, you will have in your group people who are able to do all of these things, in addition to people who can type or draw. They can help club members who are not as talented in the preparation of their displays.

Once you have decided to have a show, select a date. It usually is best to pick a weekend or a Sunday afternoon if you are only going to have a small show. Watch the calendar for other events which might be competing on the date you select. The Saturday or Sunday after Christmas or Thanksgiving are not good dates since school is out and many families will be visiting outside the area. This means you risk losing not only potential visitors to your show but potential exhibitors as well. Avoid the days which are taken up by sporting events, whether they be national or local school games.

Now, pick a place to have the show. The local library could be a good starting point. Most libraries have meeting rooms which they probably would be willing to let you use for the show.

Enlist the help of one or more adults. You probably will need their assistance in getting permission to use the room and in assuring the librarian that the show will be conducted in an orderly fashion.

Determine how many displays you are going to have and how they are going to be exhibited. You may want to put all the displays on posters and hang them on the walls. You might want to use tables on which you can open albums and display pages. The library may have a display case which can be locked and which could be used to display more valuable items.

Talk with the local postmaster about help he can give you with the show. He will be able to provide some display posters, pamphlets on collecting, and information about collector items sold by the Postal Service. He also can be helpful in borrowing a film about stamps for you from the Postal Service. The librarian can arrange for you to have the use of a projector and probably will be glad to provide someone to run it for you without cost.

Make some posters telling about the show and hang them in the library a couple of weeks ahead of time. Ask the librarian to announce your show in the bulletins put out by the library. Be sure to have posters in your school and ask your teachers to announce the news about the show.

The displays should be fairly simple. You might have one which tells how to send for first-day covers, and another which shows the difference between commemoratives and regular issues. There could be pages on topical collecting and displays of the tools used by collectors. A display could even consist of one stamp, with an explanation of when and why it was issued.

Club members should be urged to inject bits of their personality into the exhibits they prepare. At a stamp show, your album will attract more attention if you have done something to make the cover and the pages look unusual. Notice which displays win at the hobby shows. It is not always the biggest or the most expensive collection that takes the blue ribbon. Often it is the one which looks a little different from the others. The judges may look at many collections, all of which are about equal in content. The decision as to which is best often depends on which the judges believe got a little extra attention and showed use of imagination by the collector.

Ask your local stamp dealer to provide something to display at the show. He also may volunteer to donate a door prize.

Try to have one theme or idea and stick with it throughout the show. You might focus on U. S. issues and talk about all of the ways in which they can be collected. One show might be devoted to topicals, with ideas on how to mount them in unusual patterns.

Be sure that each visitor to the show signs up at the door. This gives you a list of potential members for your club who can be contacted after the show is over.

Be sure that some members of the club are present in the show area at all times. This provides protection for the displays. It also gives you a chance to meet other collectors who might want to join your club. Be especially nice to the newcomers and the younger collectors. Remember, it was not too long ago that you were finding your way into the hobby.

Send a note to the local newspaper, particularly if they have a stamp column, telling them you are planning to have a show. Invite the person who writes the column to attend.

When the show is over, be sure that all of the displays are returned to the persons who made them. Send a thank-you note to all of the people who helped put on the show. Make plans to contact the people who signed up at the door. Find out what they collect and help them meet other collectors with similar interests.

Stamp shows are fun, particularly the ones you put together yourself. By the time the first show is over you will find yourself planning for the next show and each will be bigger and better than the one before.

12
Stamp
Production

If your travels ever bring you to Washington, D.C., be sure to visit the Bureau of Engraving and Printing. This will give you a chance to get a bird's-eye view of the processes by which both our stamps and our currency are produced. "Bird's-eye view" is an appropriate term since you will be walking along catwalks which are above the equipment and will be looking down at the workers for the most part. You will see people, machines and stacks of stamps and currency beyond anything you might imagine.

The presses and the people who run them are versatile, and both work on a variety of jobs. However, the presses which print money are not used in the production of stamps. This is because currency requires deeper engravings and currency paper is harder than stamp paper, so a separate process is required for each.

As a new collector it is not essential that you be familiar with all the steps that go into stamp production. A general awareness of them, however, will make it easier for you to understand the differences in stamps and to appreciate the great effort which goes into producing them.

Three kinds of printing are used in the production of stamps. Typography, or letterpress, is the process in which the image stands out from the plate and is coated with ink before being pressed against the paper; in intaglio the image to be reproduced is cut into the plate and the ink flows into the recesses; and in offset the image is lifted from the plate by a chemical rather than a mechanical process.

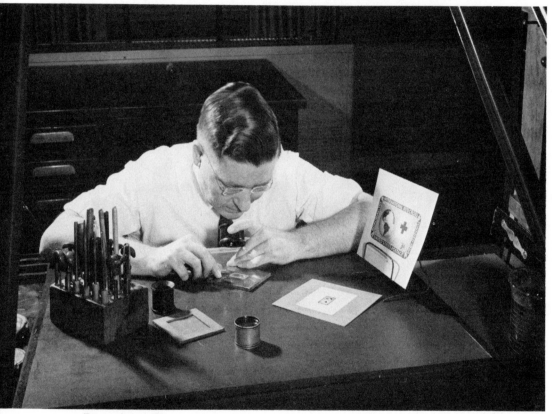

Preparing a Die

Skilled craftsmen are involved in every step of stamp production. This worker is preparing a die for the three-cent stamp which is one of several honoring the Red Cross.

Perhaps the best-known process is intaglio, frequently called recess printing. This is a method in which the design is engraved below the surface of the printing plate. The ink runs into the sunken lines and then dampened paper is forced down into the lines to pick up an impression.

The process begins with skilled engravers working from the approved art provided by the Postal Service. They cut the design in a mirror image on a flat piece of soft steel. The result is known as a die. They work with magnifying glasses and

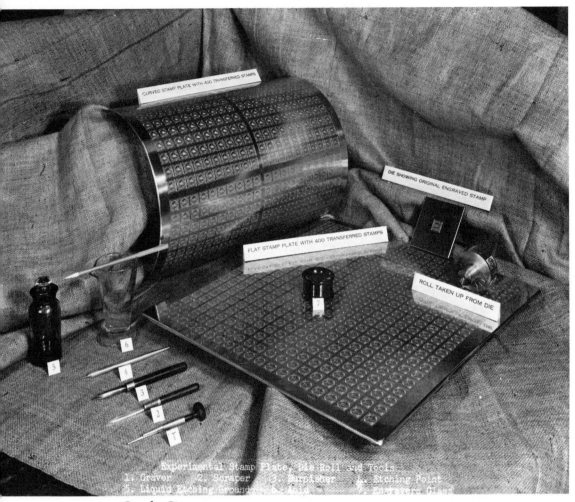

CURVED STAMP PLATE WITH 400 TRANSFERRED STAMPS

DIE SHOWING ORIGINAL ENGRAVED STAMP

FLAT STAMP PLATE WITH 400 TRANSFERRED STAMPS

ROLL TAKEN UP FROM DIE

Experimental Stamp Plate, Die Roll and Tools
1. Graver   2. Scraper   3. Burnisher   4. Etching Point
5. Liquid Etching Ground   6. Acid   7. Engraver's Glass

Step by Step

This display shows some of the special tools used and some of the steps involved in the production of United States stamps.

every detail of the design is checked repeatedly. After an acceptable engraving has been made, the die is hardened. The hardened die is next put on a transfer press and brought under pressure against a roller of soft steel. The die is rocked back and forth under increasing pressure until the soft steel is forced into the engraved lines of the die. This causes a raised surface known as a relief to appear on the roller. Ordinarily one such relief is created at a time. The process is repeated until the desired number of impressions has been created on the roller which is then hardened.

The hardened roller with the reliefs now is brought against a piece of soft steel and this forms the plate from which the stamps ultimately will be printed. A typical plate will have four hundred stamps on it, but the number will vary depending on the size and shape of the stamps. The design began in reverse on the die, was in normal position on the transfer roller, was reversed again on the printing plate and will appear normal on the finished stamps.

The plate is checked and rechecked, cleaned and polished, hardened, and bent to the curve of a cylinder if it is to be used on a rotary press. Each plate is identified by a number. This number appears on the finished panes and creates the plate number blocks valued by collectors.

The Huck Press, which combines the intaglio and offset processes, was designed especially for the Bureau and is used in the production of most modern U.S. stamps. It can print up to nine colors, with six colors applied on one unit and three colors on the other. It was put into service in 1968 and first used to produce the 1968 Christmas stamp and the six-cent flag coil stamps of 1969. It also was used for the ten-cent crossed flags issue of 1973. It can handle the printing of stamps to be issued in either coils or sheets.

Another process used on United States stamps is called photogravure. It is a form of intaglio. This method involves photographing the design through a very fine screen. A rough idea of the process can be obtained by looking at a picture through a window screen. The photo is etched into a metal plate where the tiny dots produced by the screen become holes which catch and hold the ink. The depth of the holes determines the amount of ink held and thus the degree of darkness of each part of the design. This ink is lifted up when the paper is pressed against the printing plate and the design is reproduced.

The Andreotti Press, introduced in 1971, is used in this process. It was first used to produce the Missouri Statehood stamp of 1971. It also was the only press in the Bureau able to handle the thick pressure-sensitive paper used on the experimental Christmas stamp of 1974. This stamp had the same kind of adhesive as that used on bumper stickers. The user had to remove a backing paper in order to apply the stamp to a letter. This stamp was not designed for general use, but was an experiment to see if the method of application would be practical for use on future stamps. Postal officials now indicate it is unlikely this method will be used again.

Presses are divided into sections called units, with one or more colors being applied as the paper passes through each of the sections.

Lithography or offset printing is another process by which

The Presses Roll

Workmen check the paper alignment on one of the huge presses at the Bureau of Engraving and Printing. There are several different kinds of presses to provide the various kinds of stamps needed.

stamps are produced. It is cheaper and much less complicated than the intaglio method. In basic lithography a design is drawn on a plate. The drawing is done in a greasy substance. The plate then is wet with a solution of acid and water. Since grease and water do not mix, the plate repels printing ink except the ink which hits the greasy lines of the design. If paper were pressed against the plate, it would produce a mirror image. To avoid this, the image first is transferred to a rubber blanket and then to the paper, so the design is printed right side up.

Two-color commemorative stamps are printed on the Harris Offset Press at the Bureau. The press also applies the phosphor coating or tagging which is used in the electronic sorting process.

Typography is a method of stamp production which is the reverse of the intaglio process described earlier. While the method is more commonly known as letterpress, most stamp literature uses the term "typographed." In typography, the parts of the design which are to appear on the stamp are left at the original level of the printing surface and the spaces between the design parts are cut away or etched away with acid. When ink is applied, it settles on the raised lines and prints the design when applied to paper under pressure. The printing plates are made by repeating the design on a roller as many times as desired. If the stamp has several colors, a separate plate is made for each color and only the parts of the design to appear in that color are raised on that particular plate. Separate plates for separate colors also are used in the other methods.

Sometimes several presses are used in combination for the production of a particularly elaborate stamp design. For instance, after one press applies the offset colors, the stamps then could go to another press for the intaglio color process, then to still another press for phosphor tagging and perforating.

Each time a stamp is moved from one press to another, the possibility for error occurs. In the early days of the Bureau, some presses were sheet fed rather than roller fed. This meant the stamps were printed on separate large flat sheets rather than continuously on paper coming from a web or roll. If a sheet was accidentally turned the wrong way when it was being moved to another press for the application of a second color, the design or colors would end up in the wrong position. This is how the famous inverted air-mail stamp of 1923 (the twenty-four-center with the airplane flying upside down) came to be produced.

The Giori Press is the only intaglio press with multicolor capabilities at the Bureau. Because of the arrangement of the rollers it can apply two or three different colors to the same stamp. It can produce up to nine colors and is used on our fanciest stamps. The Giori first was used to produce the four-cent flag stamp of 1957. This was the first stamp produced with all three colors printed at the same time. Previously a separate run was required for each color on a stamp. All stamps produced on the Giori Press are printed on pre-gummed paper.

Adhesive for postage stamps is another specialized area of stamp production. It has been a problem to the Postal Service for many years. Generally, in the past, the problem has been one of finding the proper combination of ingredients to make an acceptable gum or glue. In more recent years the problem has changed. The Postal Service, like the rest of the country, is faced with shortages of the materials it needs for its products. Cornstarch and dextrins are needed for glue. Substitutes are now being tried and as a result you will see variations in the adhesive from time to time. Look at the back of the next stamps you buy. You may find the gum on different stamps ranging in color from dark brown to transparent.

If you could go behind the scenes at the Bureau of Engraving, you would visit the room where the gum is produced. You would see one man working with huge vats of a mixture. His recipe is fairly simple. He takes five hundred pounds of powder and adds fifty-two gallons of water. He puts this into huge copper kettles where it is cooked and beaten for about two hours and then transferred to storage vats where it is kept at a temperature of 110 degrees.

The finished gum looks like pancake syrup and has about the same consistency. It is pumped continuously through a system of pipes running from the mixing room to the presses where it is applied to the stamps. This process goes on twenty-four hours a day, seven days a week. The glue is kept warm and circulating, even when the presses are stopped. If, for any reason, the pumping stopped and the mixture cooled, the pipes would fill with hardened glue and the equipment would be ruined. Emergency power supplies are on hand to keep the glue flowing even if the regular power system fails.

The entire stamp production process requires great control over temperature and humidity. If the ink is not dried fast enough, it will run and ruin the stamp design. If engraved work is allowed to get too warm, it will pick up ink from one roller to the next and carry the design over, thus producing defective stamps.

Various methods are used to dry the inks. They range from air blowing across the sheets to passing the stamps through specially designed "ovens." An exception is the Giori Press which uses several inks at the same time. A natural drying process is used; it takes forty-eight hours before the phosphor coating can be applied and twenty-four hours before the stamps can be stacked and cut.

You might think the rooms which house the giant presses

would be filled with the odors of inks and glue, but they are not. There is an exhaust system which draws off all the fumes. This is done not only for the comfort of the workers but also as a safety factor. A fume build-up could cause a fire or an explosion. It also could affect the moisture content of the paper and cause disruptions in the printing.

Perforating Machine

Sharp-eyed workers watch for errors as this machine puts in the perforations which make it possible to separate the stamps for mailing.

If you could get to take an inside tour of the Bureau, you would enter the press section through a set of double doors. You would be inside the first set before the second set would open. This makes it possible to adjust rapidly to the difference in air pressure caused by the exhaust system. It is similar to the system used in submarines.

On an ordinary tour you would see most of the steps described here, but you would view them from catwalks above the walk. Because of security rules you would not be allowed close enough to touch any of the stamps. Visitors on the actual work floor also would create a safety hazard and would interfere with production.

Perforations are placed on the sheets of stamps either as part of the press operation or by a separate perforating machine. The latter process is completely automated, with the printed rolls going in one end of the perforator and the finished stamps coming out the other end.

The process simply involves running the stamps between two rollers, the one having pins, the other indentations. The pins push down from the top and into the holes. The little pieces of paper punched out are drawn into a storage bin for burning.

An electric eye on the perforator guides the rolls of stamps to keep the perforations in the proper place. It also governs the process which slices the rolls apart for coils or booklet panes.

Whenever the electric eye detects a defect in the stamp, such as a shortage of glue or a bad perforation, a set of sharp blades drops down and cuts the stamps. At the same time black ink is sprayed on the damaged stamp. When these stamps reach the end of the process they are automatically rejected.

Inspection is a major part of the activity at the Bureau. Each piece of paper is accounted for, including the sheets damaged on the press or defective for any other reason. Inspectors work at all steps in the process, sometimes spot checking, other times looking at parts of each sheet. They look for bad printing, missed perforations, missed colors, bent or torn sheets, missing gum, and other defects which would cause the stamp to be less than perfect. At their feet are piles of stamps that would be a real find for a collector. Here is a coil strip missing perforations, here a sheet which has been bent so that the design is incomplete. None of these stamps will ever end up in an album. They are destined for a trip to the basement of the Bureau, where they will be shredded and burned.

Even the wonders of the atomic age have been brought into the checking process. The Accu-Ray is an atomic measuring device used to insure that the adhesive on stamps is of the proper thickness. It uses Beta rays to penetrate the paper at a point before the adhesive has been applied, and then again after the adhesive has been put on. The difference in measurement indicates the thickness of the gum.

Near each of the presses is a chart with inked needles drawing lines on moving rolls of paper. It looks like the heartbeat-measuring machines you see on the medical shows on television. The thickness of the paper before the gum is applied is traced by a blue line. After the gum is applied, the paper thickness is shown by a red line. The two lines have to stay within established standards. When there is too much or too little gum on the stamps, the machines sounds an alarm and also activates a control which sprays black ink on the stamps being printed. The stamps so marked are defective and will be removed from the press and destroyed.

Other meters check the degree of tension on the rolls of paper. Because of differences in humidity and temperature it is possible for the paper to stretch. Even a slight stretching could distort the design and cause defective stamps.

Despite all these precautions, errors do slip through. An ink feeder may clog and result in a missing color, or a color may slide over beyond where it was supposed to be placed. Paper can shift slightly on the press and cause the plate number to appear on a stamp instead of in the margin. Perforators may speed along while an electric eye failure goes briefly undetected. This produces stamps with perforations missing or perforations in the wrong place.

The stamps of the United States are the best produced and the most carefully inspected in the world. The machines are the most modern and the controls usually most effective. However, there is always the human element which can result in mistakes. An inspector looks away for a second; an ink tap is not completely open; a press speed is improperly adjusted. Mechanical failures affect all machines at some time. All of these things can lead to errors getting out to the public. These errors may distress the perfectionists at the Bureau, but they add still another touch of adventure and excitement for the stamp collector.

13
Stamp Design

"I though it would be nice to have a stamp showing a man on a horse going through a town yelling, 'Colorado is one hundred years old.' " This is just one of the letters the Citizens Stamp Advisory Committee found in its mailbox recently. It came from a student in Colorado and was one of thousands of suggestions for stamps to be issued that the U.S. Postal Service gets each year.

Like all of the other suggestions received, the Colorado stamp idea will be screened by a panel before being presented to the advisory committee, but probably the stamp never will come into being, at least not in the form suggested. The Postal Service has a series of strict rules governing the selection of subjects to appear on stamps. Since only a very limited number can be issued each year, it is easy to see why a careful screening of suggestions is needed.

The Citizens Stamp Advisory Committee is made up of eleven members. They represent historians, artists, businessmen and even stamp collectors. They meet for one or two days four times a year. It is their job to go over all of the suggestions for stamps and pick out the ones they feel would be most appropriate. It takes a long time for a stamp to go from the idea stage to the point where it is on sale at the post office. This means the stamp advisory unit has to work far ahead, sometimes as much as several years.

The committee also looks over the designs for possible stamps which have been sent in. They do not make the final selection. The recommendations go to the Office of Stamps where they are reviewed again, and then the most suitable suggestions are sent to the postmaster general for his final ruling on which will be used.

Many factors go into the selection of a subject and design for a stamp. There are general rules, which we will discuss later, but there are also special considerations. For instance, there is the question of whether a stamp will attract the attention of collectors. In the chapter about special kinds of collecting (Chapter Six) we talked about topicals—stamps with a theme. The Postal Service knows, for instance, that a stamp showing animals will attract the interest of many collectors. A stamp showing music or space or Scouts probably will be bought by many people who are not stamp collectors but who are interested in the subjects shown on the stamps.

When all of these factors have been considered, an artist is commissioned to produce a drawing of the proposed stamp.

Stamp Designs
The Postal Service gets thousands of suggestions for stamp designs. This sample was submitted to Postmaster General James A. Farley by Shirley Temple when she was a child star.

This drawing, along with all of the reasons why the stamp should be issued, plays a major part in the final decision. While many collectors send in drawings of what they would like to see on a stamp, it is very seldom that such a drawing is accepted in the form in which it is submitted. The Postal Service generally finds it best to depend on the work of a professional artist. Artists who design stamps are paid a small fee, but they get a bigger reward in the form of national recognition as a stamp designer. Many designers have several stamps to their credit.

In 1963 the Postal Service accepted a design for a Christmas stamp produced by Lily Spandorf. It showed the national Christmas tree and the White House. This was one of the few times the Postal Service has accepted work submitted by an outsider.

Before you think about sending your stamp ideas to the postmaster general, here are a few of the Postal Service rules you need to know.

No living person will be shown on any United States postage stamp. All postage stamps honoring individuals will be issued preferably on significant anniversaries of their birth, and not earlier than ten years after their death. There are exceptions to this rule. Ordinarily a memorial stamp is issued shortly after the death of a president or former president.

Commemorative postage stamps of historical significance are considered for issuance on even-date anniversaries, preferably starting with the fiftieth year and continuing a fifty-year intervals. The various statehood anniversary stamps are examples of this. The young man who required the one hundredth anniversary stamp may get his wish, but it probably won't include his shouting horseman riding through the towns.

Only themes and events of widespread national appeal and significance are considered as subjects for commemorative stamps. Many of the requests which go to the stamp advisory committee deal with subjects of purely local interest, so they are rejected.

The Postal Service bans stamps honoring fraternal, political or sectarian organizations, a commercial enterprise or a specific product. Every time you read a rule like this it is easy to think of instances where the rule has been violated. The Veterans of Foreign Wars and the Disabled American Veterans and the American Legion all are fraternal groups, yet they appeared on U.S. stamps. The Baltimore and Ohio Railroad is a

Scarce Items

*Round stamps are scarce,
but they do exist. Here are a
couple of values from a set
issued by Tonga in the
Polynesian Islands.*

commercial enterprise, as is the Montgomery Ward Company. Yet the B&O had a stamp of its own and Montgomery Ward was the subject of the mail order stamp. Clearly there are exceptions even to Postal Service rules.

Commemorative stamps are not considered appropriate for charitable organizations, even though we have several Red Cross stamps. The Postal Service feels that slogan cancellations, posters and labels are more appropriate than stamps for such endeavors.

Perhaps the United States will come around to using semipostals in the future, and this will solve the problems for at least some of the charitable organizations. This, however, does not seem likely in the foreseeable future.

Commemorative stamps are not issued for cities, towns, municipalities, countries, schools or institutions of higher learning. This is true in part because so many are reaching anniversaries that are primarily of local or regional significance rather than of national interest. Once again there are exceptions, the Columbia University stamp being one, and the Land Grant Colleges stamp another.

If you are not discouraged by the rules and still would like to submit your ideas or drawings for a proposed stamp, feel free to do so. Send your suggestions to the postmaster general, whose address appears on page 130, at least eighteen months in advance of the proposed date of issue of the stamps you suggest. This allows time for consideration by the committee and for design and production if the stamp is approved. For a free copy of a booklet outlining the rules for stamp selection, write to the U.S. Stamp Information Service, whose address is listed on page 130.

While the Postal Service admits it very rarely accepts a design proposal from an unsolicited source, it does encourage the public to contribute ideas for new stamps. School teachers often hold discussions with their classes about postage stamp designs and then the classes come up with proposed designs which are submitted to the Postal Service. The groups get a letter from the Postal Service and the designs are screened for consideration by the stamp advisory committee.

The imagination displayed by the young would-be stamp designers is interesting. A recent submission from a class in Texas included a sketch of two cats seated on a fence with the moon in the background. Across the bottom of the stamp were the words "Music in the Moonlight." The designer didn't say what the stamp was supposed to commemorate.

A ten-year-old from Seattle came out in support of a stamp for a children's favorite. He wrote: "Would like to have you issue a ten-cent Teddy Bear Stamp. The Teddy Bear has been the symble (the spelling is his) of children's toys for hundreds of years. The children of this country want a Teddy Bear stamp."

In 1964 *Look* magazine carried a story about stamp designs sent to the Postal Service by young people. They included a description of a design by a San Francisco high school student, Richard Burkley, who was fifteen at the time. The design was for the John F. Kennedy stamp and bore a remarkable resemblance to the stamp which finally was issued honoring the late president. The design never was seen by the stamp advisory committee and the Postal Service called the resemblance a "coincidence."

14
What the Postal Service Has to Offer

The United States Postal Service stands ready to help you with your stamp collecting in a variety of ways. This is true whether you are an individual collector working alone, a student in a school group, or a member of an organized philatelic club or society.

While this help is readily available, it may be necessary for you to ask for it before you can take advantage of it. The nature and amount of help you can get will depend in part on the size of the community in which you live. If you are in a metropolitan area, your post office may have a philatelic sales window or even a postal store. If you live in a small town the postal clerk may handle philatelic assignments along with his or her regular duties.

Let's take a look at some of the kinds of help that is available and how you go about getting it. Begin with your local post office. You will notice that it has a number of posters on the wall which tell which new stamps are for sale. It probably also has a wall case containing copies of each of the more recent issues. It may have one of the rotating display stands which show the various types of kits and other philatelic products offered at the counter.

The posters are colorful and interesting. They would make a nice addition to your stamp corner at home. When they are sent to a post office they are designed for display for only a short period of time, generally while the subject stamp is on sale. After that they are taken down and discarded. If you see a poster you like, ask the clerk when it is to be taken down, and if it could be put on one side for you. About a day or two before the poster is due to come down, go back to the post office and remind the clerk of your request to have the poster saved. There is no charge and the clerk probably will be happy to give it to you.

In seeking help from postal clerks, follow the same rules outlined for seeking help from stamp dealers. First, go at a time when the clerk is not busy. If there is a long line at the stamp window, you are not likely to get much cooperation. A good time to go might be on your way home from school. By then the business customers are through with their post office business for the day and the other people have not yet returned home from work.

Postal clerks are being given training in philatelic matters. The clerks in the biggest offices are receiving it faster, but all postal clerks eventually will have at least the basic information. This means it should be possible for you to ask the clerk to show you examples of a regular stamp, a commemorative, a coil stamp, a booklet pane and several kinds of postal stationery. They also can show you some of the special philatelic material they have for sale.

The postal merchandisers, those plastic containers on a revolving base, now are found in the lobbies of more than 8,500 post offices. They contain collector kits and other philatelic items. However, it is not possible for you to examine them before purchase. Check with the clerks when they are not busy and they may have an opened kit which they can show you.

The kits are a major part of the philatelic program. There currently are about a dozen varieties either on sale or in production. Originally they were called "starter" kits, but the word *starter* was dropped because some collectors complained that there were no U.S. stamps in some of the kits.

Basically, they are introductions to topical collecting. Typical of the current offerings is the "Masterwork" kit. It is in a sealed package with a picture of a cowboy on the cover. The cowboy is from a "Masterwork" painting by Frederic Remington.

In the kit are forty-three world-wide stamps, all genuine and all different. They feature reproductions of famous works of art from museums around the world. There is a twenty-page album which has spaces for each of the stamps in the kit, plus additional spaces for stamps on the same topic. In all there is room for fifty-seven stamps. An insert sheet provides space for adding even more stamps. There is a packet of hinges and a thirty-two page booklet on *The ACBs of Stamp Collecting*. The kit also includes an envelope addressed to the Philatelic Sales Division of the Postal Service and an order form for other kits in the series.

Kits offered are: Space, and a second edition on the same subject; Sports and the World of Sports; Wildlife; the Animal Kingdom; Birds and Butterflies; European Art; United States; and Canada. The albums in each of the kits have been punched to fit a three-ring binder.

Such an inexpensive binder is available from the Postal Service. It holds up to ten of the twenty-page albums. The booklet on stamp collecting is a part of each kit, so you will build up an accumulation of them if you buy more than one kit. Give your extras to friends—it could get them started on the hobby.

Another item which will be of interest and value to you as a new collector is the latest edition of *Stamps and Stories*, the pocket-size book which tells the story of more than two thousand stamps with illustrations. It is updated periodically to keep it current.

The Postal Service also offers mint sets of stamps for each year shortly after the end of the year. The price of the sets varies depending on the number of stamps issued during that year.

Among other items the Postal Service is considering for sale are the huge commemorative posters. These may be offered through a subscription service. This means you would make a deposit ahead of time to cover the cost of a number of posters and they would be sent to you as they were released. Some foreign countries sell their new issue stamps in this manner. You make a minimum deposit, generally twenty dollars, and they send you each new stamp as it comes out. When the amount of the deposit is nearly used up, they write and request more money.

We have been talking about an individual collector going into the post office and buying these items over the counter. If your post office does not have the items in stock that you want, or if it is not convenient for you to get to the post office, you can order by mail, from the Philatelic Sales Division of the U.S. Postal Service. The address is on page 130. Tell them what you want and include a money order to cover the cost. You must add fifty cents per order as a handling charge. By sending a stamped, self-addressed envelope to the same address, you can get a list of recent stamps still available at face value. They will include an order blank and rules for buying.

As a student member of a group at school you can get still more help with your collecting. You may need to enlist the aid of your teacher, but it is worth the effort.

If you have a stamp club at school you are off to a good start. If you don't have a club, get one organized as outlined elsewhere in this book. Ask one of the teachers to serve as moderator. A teacher can request the use of films about the Postal Service. This can be done through the local postmaster. If the postmaster does not have the forms or know the rules for borrowing the films, he or she can easily get them from the nearest regional office of the Postal Service.

One of the best films is a color and sound film called *Stamps, A Nation's Calling Cards*. It is designed for use with 16-millimeter projectors, the kind available in most schools. This film runs for nineteen minutes. It portrays stamps as they reflect our nation's history and heritage. Featuring the Apollo Moon Landing stamp, the film shows the process by which stamps are produced, from the first hand-engraved impression of a single stamp through the procedures that result in the final printing of millions of copies. If your teacher would like to show this film to the class, it is available on loan without charge by writing to National Audio Visual Center (GSA), whose address is listed on page 130.

The film just described is only one of the many films and filmstrips available dealing with philatelic subjects. Write to the same address, tell them the type of projection equipment your school has and they will tell you what is available.

The Postal Service wants to work closely with the schools. To that end it is designing a number of easy-to-use teaching kits. A typical kit is "The Post Rider." It contains a poster showing the four eight-cent stamps saluting the Rise of the Spirit of Independence. These 1973 stamps show the post rider, the posting of a handbill, the printing of a pamphlet and a colonial drummer. There are six plastic cards which tell the story of the broadsides, America's first newspapers. These broadsides were big sheets on which the news was printed. They were nailed up in a prominent place in town so that they could be seen by all the citizens. The plastic cards telling about them are designed to be passed around in the class. Also in the kit are "ditto masters" for reproducing the outlines of the stamps. The class then can color the pictures or use them as posters for meeting announcements or similar purposes. In each kit is a film strip with colonial scenes and a cassette recording in which a narrator talks about the various events. Completing the set is a teacher's guide with instructions on how to introduce the various parts of the kit to the class.

If you are a member of an organized stamp club you can get still further help from the Postal Service. Begin by being sure that the local postmaster is aware of the existence of your club. Tell him about your meetings and invite him to attend a session. Find out if he is a collector or if any of the clerks in his office collect. You might be able to get one of them to appear as a speaker at your club. Arrange with the postmaster for a tour of the postal facility. Do this far enough in advance so that he can schedule your visit when the office is not too busy and he can arrange to have a guide for you. If your club is part of a school activity, you might be able to schedule the visit as a field trip during regular class hours.

To really enjoy stamp collecting you need to do more than just put stamps in an album. It helps to know something about the history of the Postal Service and about the way mail is handled. It may come as a surprise to you to learn that in many post offices today the mail still is processed in the same way it was back in the days of Benjamin Franklin. In others, the most modern electronic equipment speeds the sorting and dispatch of letters. Find out which you have in your community. Your postmaster also can arrange for you a visit a sectional center, the large facility which handles the mail from many post offices.

The Postal Service people are going to be eager to help with your stamp collecting activities. Some of them will be eager because they like to work with young people or are interested in stamp collecting and stamp collectors. The others will be encouraged to be interested since the postal service will be stressing philatelic sales.

AMERICAN BAL ...LE

Stamp Collecting U.S. 8¢

U.S. 6¢

HAIDA CEREMONIAL CANOE

15
The Young Collector

The new collector has many advantages. You begin with a wide open world. There are many thousands of stamps you can acquire before you need to begin making major investments in your collection.

Every stamp you encounter in the early stages is an opportunity to fill a space or begin developing a trading stock. You are able to buy the large packets and spend many happy hours sorting through them. You are free to experiment in large areas of collecting, delaying any firm decision until you have had many months to decide what and how you want to collect.

At several points in the book we have talked about how ingenuity and imagination add to your enjoyment of the hobby. This is particularly true when you are a new collector. This ingenuity can be demonstrated in the way you design your album pages, or even in the way you dress them up if you use the regular printed pages. It can show up in the way you make cachets for your first-day covers and in the way you prepare an exhibit for a stamp show. It can be seen in stamp design compettitions and in posters and signs advertising the meetings of your stamp club.

After you have been collecting for a little while you will want to do things which will personalize your collection and make it stand out from those around it.

Here are some ideas on how to add a personal touch to your stamp collection.

Try to get first-day covers on all of the U. S. stamps which have come out during your lifetime. Most of these covers still are available through stamp dealers. Begin with the oldest issues since they will be hardest to get. A look at your stamp catalog will tell you which stamps were issued, where and when they came out. You might want to copy this list into a loose-leaf notebook and use it as a check list, crossing off each stamp or cover as you add it to your collection. Let your friends and relatives know what you are planning and they may decide to fill some of the blank spaces for you as birthday or holiday gifts.

Give a list of the covers you need to several stamp dealers in your area and ask them to call you if they get any of the ones you need. When collections are sold they often include at least a few covers. One or more of these covers may be on your want list. A dealer who buys such a collection will remember that you are looking for certain covers and will notify you when he gets them.

If you don't want to collect the covers, you might want to try and get mint or used copies of all the U.S. stamps which came out during your lifetime. Begin by writing to the Philatelic Sales Agency, of the U.S. Postal Service, whose address is on page 130. Send them a stamped, self-addressed en-

Youthful Heroine
On the dark night of April 26, 1777, 16-year-old Sybil Ludington rode her horse "Star" alone through the Connecticut countryside rallying her father's militia to repel a raid by the British on Danbury. This stamp is part of the "Contributors to the Cause" series issued in 1975.

velope and they will send you a list of the stamps available and an order blank. In this way you can get stamps of at least the last couple of years at face value plus a small service charge. Go back again to your friend the stamp dealer and tell him the stamps you need to complete your "lifetime" collection. He probably will have most of them in stock and his price list will tell you what it will cost to get the stamps you want. You then can budget your purchases.

Once you have begun a collection of this type, be sure to keep it current by getting new issues as they appear. The weekly stamp columns and other philatelic publications will tell you well in advance when a new stamp is coming out.

The same idea can be expanded to include plate blocks, blocks of four or any other combination of stamps you choose to collect.

An even more personalized collection can be made by linking the stamps and covers you have to special events in your life. This probably will require you to create your own album, but this adds to the enjoyment. You could begin with a stamp from the area in which you were born. Statehood stamps are readily available and are ideal for this purpose. If you moved to another state, you could add a stamp or cover showing its anniversary.

Presidents were elected during your lifetime so you could include covers carrying cachets about them. Presidents may have died during your lifetime and they appear on stamps which would fit into a collection of this type.

Vacation trips give you an opportunity to add to this special collection. If you visit a national park, there are several stamps which show the various parks. State stamps again can be used to show places you have visited. Make notes on the pages to remind you of special happenings and dress up the page with a photo or a sticker such as the kind people sometimes put on their suitcases to show they have visited a certain area.

Those of you who are active in Boy or Girl Scouts have many chances to add philatelic items to your collection which can be linked to scouting. There is everything from a stamp honoring each of the Scout groups to one showing George Washington at Valley Forge, site of national Scout jamborees.

This kind of an album can be developed over many years. When you go off to college, there are stamps showing famous educators whose work you may be studying, artists, poets, painters and writers you admire. A collection of this type could become a kind of family history which could be passed down through generations just like an old family Bible.

When you have this kind of collection, it makes your display stand out at a stamp or hobby show. It gives you an excellent subject for a talk in school or at a stamp club, and it provides you with interesting contacts with people who will want to help you build the collection. Such an album could be the start of a family hobby that would involve family members of all ages.

Your class at school might want to take on an album of this type as a school project and develop it into a collection which would become part of the school library. It could house stamps which deal with events which are important to the school. The school, for instance, might be named after a president. The collection could begin with stamps and covers showing the president so honored. The section on sports could carry items about school athletes and could be surrounded by the football, baseball and basketball stamps issued by the United States. The clippings about musical achievements of the students could include the American Music stamp and stamps from the Famous American series showing composers. This same approach could be carried over into all phases of school activity.

Another school project could involve having your stamp club join in the observance of National Stamp Collecting Week. This usually comes about the middle of November and often is marked by the issue of a new stamp or piece of postal stationery. You might want to order first-day covers of the stamp issued during National Stamp Collecting Week. Chapter Seven on first-day covers outlines the procedure to follow.

Students who go through the process of sending for one of the first-day covers may just become enough interested in collecting to decide to enter the hobby. In this way you will have a chance to add yet another member to your club.

In the chapter on stamp clubs you learned how contests and other special activities can keep a club going and how such activities can be used in a program like the one we are talking about here.

The longer you collect the more you will want to do things which will make your collection stand out from those around it. In this chapter we have given you some ideas on how this can be done. You probably can think of many more. Next time you open your album, think not only of putting in another stamp, but add a touch of your own personality.

16
What Next?

By now you have mastered the basic steps of collecting. You understand some of the technical language and you are beginning to have definite ideas of what and how you want to collect. You must now decide the direction and the pace at which you want to go in the immediate future and for your long-range hobby activities.

Hopefully by this time you have joined a stamp club or at least checked out a few in your area. Even if you do not feel the need of having others around when you are working on your collection, there still are many advantages in belonging to a club. Just the awareness of changes going on in the collecting world makes club membership worth the time and money.

If you prefer to be a loner, then you will want to develop a philatelic library and some contact with mail order dealers as a means of getting the supplies and information you need.

You can begin your library with a few items from the Government Printing Office. The first of these is the book,

Postage Stamps of the United States. This is a comprehensive review of all U.S. postage stamps from the first adhesive of 1847 through the six-cent Natural History commemoratives of May 1970. It contains black and white illustrations of the stamps, with detailed information as to why each stamp was issued, its exact dimensions and color, when and where it was first placed on sale. In addition to stamps, the book has information on postal cards, stamped envelopes and related items. It tells the number of stamps printed for each commemorative issue and the number of plates used in printing them. Designers and engravers are listed for each stamp issued since 1933. There also is special information on first-day covers. The GPO catalog number is P4.10:970.

Supplemental Reading
Stamp publications increase your enjoyment and understanding of the hobby. They come in many shapes and sizes. Write the publishers for a sample copy and then decide which you like best.

To supplement this information you will want *Transmittal Letter 2, Postage Stamps of the United States.* This contains the first additions to the 1970 edition and it also makes minor corrections to that edition. The listing starts with the Maine Statehood commemorative of 1970 and concludes with the 1971 Christmas stamps which were issued in November 1971. The GPO catalog number is P4.10:Trans. 2.

The small commemorative stamp posters also are available from the Government Printing Office. They come out three or four weeks ahead of the issue date of a new stamp. In addition to an enlarged photo of the stamp, the 8″ x 10½″ posters provide other data of interest to stamp collectors, such as the date and place of issue, name of designer, number of copies to be printed, size and color. Each poster also includes complete instructions on sending for first-day covers. The GPO catalog number is P1.26/2:(CSP).

Orders for the books described above or for the posters should be sent to the Superintendent of Documents, Government Printing Office, whose address is on page 130. You can obtain current prices too. You must include the GPO number as a means of identifying the publications you want.

You ought to seriously consider subscribing to a stamp publication. It will keep you current on new issues and also will alert you to other happenings in the philatelic world. There are a number of good stamp publications. Most of the publishers will be happy to send you a sample free or at a very small cost.

A few of the publications to which you might want to write for sample copies and subscription information are listed on page 130.

While you are writing for samples of publications, you might want to write to some of the philatelic organizations and find out what they have to offer. The names and addresses of some of the major national organizations are on page 130.

There are also dozens of smaller specialized societies. Inquire at the stamp club or at your library. They will have some stamp publications and can refer you to others which might be of specific interest to you.

Try not to limit your collecting, particularly in the early days of your entry into the hobby. To do so could cut you out of some interesting contacts with stamps and stamp collectors.

Periodically you will want to take a close look at your collection and set some goals. You may decide you want to get all the stamps prior to a certain date, or all the stamps of a certain country.

Keep open the option of moving into topicals or some other general area. This gives you some place to go when it becomes too expensive to add stamps to your current collection.

Expand your enjoyment of the hobby by sharing it with others. As your knowledge and understanding of stamps increase, pass along some of the information to others who might become interested in the hobby.

If you have a flair for writing, you could become a part-time philatelic writer. You could begin by doing a stamp column for your school paper. The Postal Service will provide you with information on new issues or you can get it from the posters in the post office. You might even get a chance to do a column for junior collectors in your local weekly newspaper. Write a letter to the editor, send him a sample of the kind of column you would write and see if he is interested.

Finally, begin early in your collecting career to treat your stamp collection as the important and valuable piece of property it is. Know what stamps you have—keep an inventory of them. Know what stamps you need in the areas you want to pursue—develop a want list of them. Read stamp literature and get active in stamp groups. The more interest and effort you put into the hobby, the more excitement and enjoyment you will get out of it.

Many years from now, when you are introducing your grandchildren to the wonders of stamp collecting, you will remember with pleasure the early days of your collecting which started you on the hobby that is designed to last a lifetime.

Happy collecting!

Useful Names
and Addresses

National Audio Visual Center (GSA), Washington, D.C. 20409.
Philatelic Sales Agency, U.S. Postal Service, Washington, D.C. 20044.
Philatelic Sales Division, U.S. Postal Service, Washington, D.C. 20036.
Postmaster General, Washington, D.C. 20260.
Superintendent of Documents, Government Printing Office, Washington, D.C. 20402.
U.S. Stamp Information Service, Office of Stamps, Box 764, Washington, D.C. 20044.

National Philatelic Organizations

American Philatelic Society, Box 800, State College, PA 16801.
American Topical Association, 3308 N. 50th Street, Milwaukee, WI 53216.
Bureau Issues Association, 19 Maple Street, Arlington, MA 02174.
Society of Philatelic Americans, Box 42060, Cincinnati, OH 45242.
United Postal Stationery Society, Box 1407, Bloomington, IL 61701.

Philatelic Publications

Linn's Weekly Stamp News, Box 29, OH 45365.
Mekeel's Weekly Stamp News, Box 1660, Portland, ME 04104.
Minkus Stamp Journal, 116 West 32nd Street, New York, NY 10001.
Bill Olcheski's Stamp Newsletter for Collector Families, Box 30, Falls Church, VA 22046.
Scott Monthly Journal, 10102 F Street, Omaha, NE 68127.
Stamp Newsletter for Collector Families, Box 30, Falls Church, VA 22046.
Stamps, 153 Waverley Place, New York, NY 10014.
Western Stamp Collector, Box 10, Albany, OR 97321.

Index